Ayad Akhtar

The Invisible Hand

Bloomsbury Methuen Drama
An imprint of Bloomsbury Publishing Plc

BLOOMSBURY
LONDON · OXFORD · NEW YORK · NEW DELHI · SYDNEY

Bloomsbury Methuen Drama

An imprint of Bloomsbury Publishing Plc

50 Bedford Square	175 Fifth Avenue
London	New York
WC1B 3DP	NY 10010
UK	USA

www.bloomsbury.com

Bloomsbury is a registered trade mark of Bloomsbury Publishing Plc

First published in 2015 in the USA by Little, Brown & Company
First published by Methuen Drama in 2016 with changes to the script

© Ayad Akhtar 2015, 2016

Published by arrangement with Hachette Book Group. All rights reserved.

British Library Cataloguing-in-Publication Data
A catalogue record for this book is available from the Library of Congress

ISBN: PB: 978-1-3500-1350-6
ePDF: 978-1-3500-1351-3
ePub: : 978-1-3500-1352-0

Library of Congress Cataloging-in-Publication Data
A catalog record for this book is available from the Library of Congress

Typeset by Country Setting, Kingsdown, Kent CT14 8ES
Printed and bound in Great Britain

Tricycle Theatre presents

The Invisible Hand

by
Ayad Akhtar

Originally produced by
THE REPERTORY THEATRE OF ST. LOUIS
Steven Woolf, Artistic Director
Mark Bernstein, Managing Director

First performed in the UK by the
TRICYCLE THEATRE, LONDON
on 12 May 2016

Tricycle Theatre

A local theatre with an international presence

The Tricycle views the world through a variety of lenses, bringing unheard voices into the mainstream. It presents high-quality and innovative work which provokes debate and emotionally engages. Located in Brent, the most diverse borough in London, the Tricycle is a local venue with an international vision.

Recent Tricycle productions include *The Mother* and *The Father* (Molière Award-winner, West End/UK tour) by Florian Zeller, the UK premiere of *A Wolf In Snakeskin Shoes* and *The House That Will Not Stand* by Marcus Gardley, *Multitudes* by John Hollingworth, the Olivier Award-winning *Handbagged* by Moira Buffini (West End/UK tour), *Paper Dolls* by Philip Himberg and *Red Velvet* by Lolita Chakrabarti (West End/New York, winner of two Critics' Circle Awards and an Evening Standard Award).

The Tricycle has recently collaborated with Sundance Theatre Lab, Complicite, Frantic Assembly, Birmingham Rep, Tiata Fahodzi, Paines Plough, Liverpool Everyman, Eclipse Theatre, Theatre Royal Bath, Why Not Theatre and Theatre Royal Plymouth, amongst others.

Our ambitious Creative Learning programme aims to develop the imagination, aspiration and potential of children and young people. We invest in creating meaningful relationships with young people who are passionate about theatre but often have limited access to it.

 /tricycletheatre

 @tricycletheatre

www.tricycle.co.uk

Welcome from the Director

Ayad had come to my attention via his Pulitzer Prize award-winning play, *Disgraced*, though I had never met him. Then just over a year ago a colleague sent me a play they thought I would love. As soon as I read *The Invisible Hand* I was struck by how engaging and timely the piece was. I immediately began working out when we could programme it. I knew I wanted to bring it to the Tricycle.

Ayad and I finally met last July in Utah, where we were both working at Sundance Theatre Lab. We immediately got on well with each other, sparring ideas and debating politics. We discussed the play and the possibility of bringing it to Kilburn. Thankfully he agreed that the Tricycle should produce the UK premiere of *The Invisible Hand*.

What I find exciting about the play is how it defies expectations. While I initially speculated this was going to be a play about terrorism and religious extremism in Pakistan, after reading the first few pages my assumptions were completely undermined. The play is both personal and universal; these characters' personal journeys are inextricably tied to big-picture politics and the global economy.

I believe that in the current worldwide climate of economic instability, Islamophobia and conflict, this play could not be more relevant in challenging our perceptions of freedom and responsibility.

It has been wonderful to work with this text full of unexpected humour and searing insight. After four weeks in a rehearsal room full of laughter, hard work and muscular debate, we look forward to sharing this experience with you. I do hope you enjoy your evening at the Tricycle Theatre and will come back and visit us soon.

Indhu

Indhu Rubasingham
Artistic Director
Tricycle Theatre

Cast
in order of appearance

Nick Bright — **Daniel Lapaine**
Dar — **Sid Sagar**
Bashir — **Parth Thakerar**
Imam Saleem — **Tony Jayawardena**

Creative Team

Director — **Indhu Rubasingham**
Designer — **Lizzie Clachan**
Lighting Designer — **Oliver Fenwick**
Sound Designer — **Alexander Caplen**
Assistant Director — **Jennifer Bakst**
Fight Directors — **Rachel Bown-Williams and Ruth Cooper-Brown** of RC Annie Ltd
Dialect Coach — **Richard Ryder**

Production Manager — **Shaz McGee**
Company Stage Manager — **Lauren Harvey**
Deputy Stage Manager — **Charlotte Padgham**
Assistant Stage Manager — **Imogen Firth**
Rehearsal ASM — **Davey Williams**
Abi Cook
Winch Operator — **Aaron Craven-Grew**
Costume Supervisor — **Johanna Coe**
Wardrobe Mistress — **Leah Curtis**
Chief Electrician — **Andy Furby**
Head of Sound — **Mike Thacker**
Lighting Board Operator — **Ben Jones**
Set built by — **Ridiculous Solutions**
Crew — **Liam Hill, Phil Atherton, Kieran Watson, Emma Hughes, Tim de Vos, Jack Dixon, Lara Davidson, Joe Crossley, Sebastian Cannings, Max Cherry**
Casting Director — **Briony Barnett**
Press Representation — **Kate Morley PR**
Photography — **Mark Douet**
Hair & Make-up Specialist — **Susanna Peretz**
Handcuffs supplied by — **www.thetwinsfx.com**

MAKE-UP PROVIDED BY
M·A·C

This production is supported by Jon and NoraLee Sedmak

Cast Biographies

Daniel Lapaine | Nick Bright

Daniel trained at NIDA in Sydney, Australia.

Theatre includes: *The Merchant of Venice* (Shakespeare's Globe); *Other Desert Cities, Hedda Gabler* (Old Vic); *The Winter's Tale* (Crucible Theatre, Sheffield); *The Dance of Death* (Donmar Warehouse); *All My Sons* (West End); *Scenes from the Back of Beyond, F***ing Games* (Royal Court); *Les Parents Terribles, King Lear* (Sydney Theatre Company); *Island* (Belvoir); *Romeo and Juliet, Richard III, Hamlet* (Bell Shakespeare).

Television includes: *Versailles, Catastrophe, Critical, Vexed, Lewis, Vera, Black Mirror, Identity, Moonshot, Hotel Babylon, Sex, the City and Me, Jane Hall, Good Housekeeping Guide, Golden Hour, Jericho, Death on the Nile, Redcap, Helen of Troy, I Saw You, Tenth Kingdom, GP, A Country Practice.*

Film includes: *Dead in Tombstone, Zero Dark Thirty, Gozo, Jack the Giant Killer, Shanghai, Last Chance Harvey, Collusion, Abduction Club, Ritual, Journeyman, Double Jeopardy, Elephant Juice, Brokedown Palace, 54, Say You'll Be Mine, 1999, Dangerous Beauty, Polish Wedding, Muriel's Wedding.*

Radio includes: *Hedda Gabler* (BBC4); *Death of a Salesman* (BBC3); *When Elvis Met The Beatles* (BBC2).

Tony Jayawardena | Imam Saleem

Theatre includes: *Bend It Like Beckham* (West End); *The Roaring Girl, Arden of Faversham, The White Devil, The Empress, Twelfth Night* (RSC); *Dick Whittington, Love and Stuff, Cinderella* (Theatre Royal Stratford East); *Wind in the Willows* (West Yorkshire Playhouse); *Wah! Wah! Girls* (Sadler's Wells/Kneehigh); *Great Expectations* (English Touring Theatre); *The Lion, the Witch and the Wardrobe* (Royal & Derngate); *London Assurance, All's Well That Ends Well, England People Very Nice* (National Theatre).

Television includes: *The Windsors, Strikeback, Cuckoo, The Life and Adventures of Nicholas Nickleby: Beautiful Day, Pete vs. Life, Kabadasses, Silent Witness, Moses Jones, Trial and Retribution, Blair, Doctors, Hotel Babylon, Holby City.*

Film includes: *A Street Cat Named Bob, The Cook, Jadoo, Trance, The Wedding Video, The Massive, Tower Block, Screwed, Huge, A Bunch of Amateurs, Chasing Liberty.*

Sid Sagar | Dar

Sid trained at the National Youth Theatre and studied at the University of Bristol.

Theatre includes: *The Tempest, Cymbeline, The Oresteia, The Taming of the Shrew* (Shakespeare's Globe); *Treasure* (Finborough Theatre); *The History Boys* (UK tour); *True Brits* (HighTide/Edinburgh/Bush Theatre); *Eternal Love* (Shakespeare's Globe/ English Touring Theatre); *Orpheus and Eurydice* (National Youth Theatre).

Film includes: *Karma Magnet.*

Television includes: *The Hollow Crown II, The Lost Honour of Christopher Jefferies.*

Parth Thakerar | Bashir

Parth trained at RADA, London.

Theatre includes: *King Charles III* (UK tour); *The Hard Problem* (National Theatre); *Arcadia* (Nottingham Playhouse); *King Lear* (Chichester Festival Theatre/ BAM).

Creative Team

Ayad Akhtar | Playwright

Theatre includes: *Disgraced* (American Theater Company, Chicago/ Lincoln Center Theater, New York – winner of the 2013 Pulitzer Prize for Drama); *The Who and the What* (La Jolla Playhouse/Lincoln Center Theater, New York).

Ayad is the author of *American Dervish*, published in over twenty languages worldwide. His stage play *Disgraced* played at New York's LCT3/Lincoln Center Theater in 2012, and won the 2013 Pulitzer Prize for Drama. *The Who and the What* premiered at La Jolla Playhouse in February 2014 and opened in New York at LCT3/Lincoln Center Theater in June 2014. He has been the recipient of fellowships from MacDowell and Yaddo, as well as commissions from Lincoln Center Theater and the Berliner Ensemble.

Indhu Rubasingham | Director

Indhu is the Artistic Director of the Tricycle Theatre.

As Artistic Director: *A Wolf In Snakeskin Shoes, Multitudes, The House That Will Not Stand, Handbagged* (Tricycle/West End – Olivier Award for Outstanding Achievement in an Affiliate Theatre, Olivier Award nominee for Best New Comedy); *Paper Dolls, Red Velvet* (Tricycle/New York/West End – Evening Standard Award and Critics' Circle Award).

For the Tricycle: *Women, Power and Politics, Stones In His Pockets, Detaining Justice, The Great Game: Afghanistan, Fabulation, Starstruck.*

Other selected directing credits include: *The Motherf**ker with the Hat, The Waiting Room* (National Theatre); *Belong, Disconnect, Free Outgoing, Lift Off, Clubland, The Crutch, Sugar Mummies* (Royal Court); *Ruined* (Almeida); *Yellowman, Anna in the Tropics* (Hampstead Theatre); *The Ramayana* (National Theatre/Birmingham Rep); *Secret Rapture, The Misanthrope, Romeo and Juliet* (Chichester Festival Theatre); *Pure Gold* (Soho Theatre); *No Boys Cricket Club, Party Girls* (Theatre Royal Stratford East); *Wuthering Heights* (Birmingham Rep); *Heartbreak House* (Watford Palace Theatre); *Sugar Dollies, Shakuntala* (Gate Theatre); *A River Sutra* (Three Mill Island Studios); *Rhinoceros* (UC Davies, California); *A Doll's House* (Young Vic).

Indhu has previously been Associate Director of the Gate Theatre, Birmingham Rep and Young Vic.

Lizzie Clachan | Designer

Theatre includes: *The Truth* (Menier Chocolate Factory); *Cyprus Avenue* (Royal Court/Abbey Theatre, Dublin); *Macbeth, A Season in the Congo, The Soldier's Fortune* (Young Vic); *As You Like It, The Beaux Stratagem, Treasure Island, Edward II, Port, A Woman Killed with Kindness* (National Theatre); *Tipping the Velvet, Contains Violence, Absolute Beginners* (Lyric Hammersmith); *The Striker* (Manchester International Festival/Royal Exchange Theatre, Manchester); *Carmen Disruption* (Almeida); *Fireworks, Adler and Gibb, Gastronauts, The Witness, Our Private Life, Wastwater, Aunt Dan and Lemon, The Girlfriend Experience, Woman and Scarecrow, Ladybird* (Royal Court); *Jumpy* (Royal Court/West End); *On Insomnia and Midnight* (Royal Court/Festival Internacional Cervantino, Guanajuato/Centro Cultural Helénico, Mexico City); *The Forbidden Zone* (Salzburg/Berlin); *All My Sons* (Regent's Park Open Air Theatre); *A Sorrow Beyond Dreams* (Burgtheater, Vienna); *Le Vin Herbe, Bliss* (Staatsoper, Berlin); *Longing, The Trial of Ubu, Tiger Country* (Hampstead Theatre); *The Rings of Saturn* (Schauspiel, Cologne); *Happy Days* (Crucible Theatre, Sheffield); *Far Away* (Bristol Old Vic); *Shoot/Get Treasure/Repeat* (Paines Plough); *I'll Be the Devil, Days of Significance, The American Pilot* (RSC); *The Architects, Money, Tropicana, Amato Saltone, Ether Frolics, Dance Bear Dance, The Ballad of Bobby Francois, The Tennis Show* (Shunt); *Bedtime Story, The End of the Beginning* (Union Theatre/Young Vic); *Julie, Gobbo*

(National Theatre of Scotland); *Factory Girls* (Arcola); *All in the Timing* (Peepolykus); *Moonstone* (Royal Exchange Theatre, Manchester); *Treasure Island* (West End).

Lizzie co-founded Shunt in 1998, and won Best Design at the Theatre Awards UK for *Happy Days*.

Oliver Fenwick | Lighting Designer

For the Tricycle: *Multitudes, Red Velvet* (also New York/West End); *Paper Dolls, Bracken Moor, Handbagged* (also West End/UK tour).

Theatre includes: *Love's Labour's Lost, Much Ado About Nothing, The Jew of Malta, Wendy and Peter Pan, The Winter's Tale, The Taming of the Shrew, Julius Caesar, The Drunks, The Grain Store* (RSC); *The Motherf**ker with the Hat, The Holy Rosenburgs, The Passion, Happy Now?* (National Theatre); *Lela & Co, Routes, The Witness, Disconnect* (Royal Court); *The Vote, Berenice, Huis Clos* (Donmar Warehouse); *My City, Ruined* (Almeida); *Di and Viv and Rose, The Importance of Being Earnest, Bakersfield Mist, The Madness of George III, Ghosts, Kean, The Solid Gold Cadillac, Secret Rapture* (West End); *To Kill a Mockingbird* (UK tour/Barbican); *The King's Speech* (UK tour); *After Miss Julie* (Young Vic); *Saved, A Midsummer Night's Dream* (Lyric Hammersmith); *To Kill a Mockingbird, Hobson's Choice, The Beggar's Opera* (Regent's Park Open Air Theatre); *Right Now, Thérèse Raquin, The Big Meal, King Lear, Candida* (Theatre Royal Bath); *The Whipping Man* (Theatre Royal Plymouth); *Into the Woods, Sunday in the Park with George* (Théâtre du Châtelet, Paris); *The Kitchen Sink, The Contingency Plan, If There is I Haven't Found It Yet* (Bush Theatre); *A Number, Travels With My Aunt* (Menier Chocolate Factory); *Reasons to Be Happy, Private Lives, The Giant, Glass Eels, Comfort Me with Apples* (Hampstead Theatre); *Restoration* (Headlong); *Pride and Prejudice, Hamlet, The Caretaker, Comedy of Errors, Bird Calls, Iphigenia* (Crucible Theatre, Sheffield).

Opera includes: *Werther* (Scottish Opera); *The Merry Widow* (Opera North/ Sydney Opera House); *Samson et Dalila, Lohengrin, The Trojan Trilogy, The Nose, The Gentle Giant* (Royal Opera House).

Alexander Caplen | Sound Designer

For the Tricycle: *Red Velvet* (associate, also New York)

Theatre Includes: *People, Places and Things* (associate), *Constellations* (associate, West End); *We Want You to Watch, Hotel, Carpe Diem, The Dorfman Opening Gala* (National Theatre); *Martyr* (Actors Touring Company/Unicorn/UK tour); *Crave, Illusions, The Golden Dragon, The Events* (Actors Touring Company/international tour/New York); *A Time to Reap, Ding Dong the Wicked, Goodbye to All That, Wanderlust* (Royal Court); *Over There* (Royal Court/Schaubühne, Berlin); *Donkey Heart* (Old Red Lion/Trafalgar Studios); *Ogres* (Tristan Bates); *It's About Time*

(Nabokov); *Mine, Ten Tiny Toes, War and Peace* (Shared Experience); *Peter Pan, Holes, Duck Variations* (UK tour); *The Wizard of Oz, The Entertainer* (Nuffield, Southampton).

Opera includes: *The Love for Three Oranges, Tosca* (Grange Park Opera).

Alex is an Associate Artist (Sound) for Actors Touring Company.

Jennifer Bakst | Assistant Director

Jennifer is Resident Director at the Tricycle Theatre.

For the Tricycle: *Handbagged* (UK tour); *A Wolf in Snakeskin Shoes, Ben Hur, The Mother.*

Directing credits include: *Armstrong's War, Hate Radio, The Flouers o' Edinburgh* (Finborough Theatre); *Pocatello* (Mountview Academy of Theatre Arts); *Letters, Signs and Songs* (charity gala for Shakespeare's Globe); *L'elisir d'amore* (Fine Arts Theatre, Atlanta, USA); *Bash* (Etcetera Theatre); *Selkie* (Southwark Playhouse); *Bong Hits for Jesus* (Theatre503); *Acis and Galatea* (Arcola Theatre); *The Collectors* (Courtyard Theatre); *Tiny Dynamite* (Cockpit Theatre); *Everything Happens at the Starlight Lounge* (Vault Festival).

Associate Directing credits include: *Dessa Rose* (Trafalgar Studios); *Love's Labour's Lost* (Unicorn Theatre/International Shakespeare Festival, Neuss); *Samson et Dalila* (Deutsche Oper Berlin).

Play translation includes: *Summer 14* (German to English, Finborough Theatre).

Jennifer was previously the Associate Director of the Finborough Theatre and Performance Programme Associate for the Mountview Academy of Theatre Arts.

Briony Barnett | Casting Director

For the Tricycle: *Ben Hur, A Wolf In Snakeskin Shoes, The House That Will Not Stand, The Colby Sisters of Pittsburgh, Pennsylvania, Handbagged* (also West End), *One Monkey Don't Stop No Show.*

Theatre includes: *A Raisin in the Sun* (Crucible Theatre, Sheffield/UK tour); *Ticking* (West End); *Play Mas* (Orange Tree); *The Royal Duchess Superstore* (The Broadway/Half Moon); *Fences* (Theatre Royal Bath/West End).

Film includes: *Zero Sum, What We Did on Our Holiday* (children), *High Tide, Travellers, The Borderlands, Stop, Janet and Bernard, Common People, The Knot, 10 by10.*

Television includes: *Dickensian* (children), *Outnumbered* (children), *Inside the Mind of Leonardo.*

Richard Ryder | Dialect Coach

For the Tricycle: *A Wolf In Snakeskin Shoes, Multitudes, The House That Will Not Stand, Paper Dolls, Red Velvet* (also West End), *The Colby Sisters of Pittsburgh, Pennsylvania.*

Theatre includes: *Harry Potter and the Cursed Child, Kinky Boots the Musical, The Elephant Man, Fatal Attraction, The Duck House, Uncle Vanya, A View from the Bridge, King Charles III, Barking in Essex, The Nether, Three Lions* (West End); *Ah, Wilderness!, Man* (Young Vic); *A Streetcar Named Desire* (Young Vic/Broadway); *East is East, Our Country's Good, Jane Eyre, Waste, One Man Two Guvnors* (UK tour); *A Taste of Honey, Blurred Lines, Protest Song, Fifty Years on Stage, Emil and the Detectives, Home, Romeo and Juliet, Untold Stories, Table, This House, Port, The Captain of Köpenick, Cocktail Sticks, Hymn* (National Theatre); *The Tempest, The Merchant of Venice* (RSC); *American Psycho, The Turn of the Screw* (Almeida); *Fings Ain't Wot They Used T'Be, Oh, What a Lovely War!* (Theatre Royal Stratford East); *Billy Liar, Wonderful Town* (Royal Exchange Theatre, Manchester); *Race, Hysteria* (Hampstead Theatre); *Love, Bombs and Apples* (Arcola/UK tour); *Road to Mecca, In Skagway, Moby Dick, but i cd only whisper* (Arcola); *Proof* (Menier Chocolate Factory); *Clybourne Park* (Mercury Theatre, Colchester); *Electra, The Winslow Boy* (Old Vic); *A Raisin in the Sun, One Monkey Don't Stop No Show* (Eclipse Theatre); *The 39 Steps* (West End/UK tour); *Anything Goes, Oliver, The History Boys, My Fair Lady, A Taste of Honey* (Crucible Theatre, Sheffield); *The Kingdom* (Soho Theatre); *Beautiful Burnout* (Frantic Assembly); *A View from the Bridge, The Norman Conquests* (Liverpool Everyman); *Twist of Gold* (Polka Theatre); *It Just Stopped* (Orange Tree); *Steel Magnolias, The Talented Mr. Ripley, September in the Rain* (Queen's Theatre, Hornchurch); *Outside Mullingar* (Ustinov Studio, Bath).

Television includes: *Raised by Wolves, Rovers, Elizabeth, Michael and Marlon, You, Me and the Apocalypse, Cradle to the Grave, Crims.*

Film includes: *Set Fire to the Stars, The Lady in the Van.*

Richard has worked in the voice departments of the RSC and the National Theatre. He has released an accent app for actors called 'The Accent Kit', a free download for iPhone and Android.

www.richardrydervoice.com / www.theaccentkit.com

Rachel Bown-Williams & Ruth Cooper-Brown *of RC-Annie Ltd*
Fight Directors

For the Tricycle: *A Wolf In Snakeskin Shoes, Once a Catholic, Bracken Moor, Paper Dolls, Red Velvet.*

Theatre includes: *Soul* (Royal & Derngate/Hackney Empire); *The Nap, Playing for Time, Blasted* (Crucible Theatre, Sheffield); *The Threepenny*

Opera, *Cleansed* (National Theatre); *Great Expectations*, *Richard III* (West Yorkshire Playhouse); *Jumpy*, *My People*, *All My Sons*, *Aristocrats*, *Salt*, *Root and Roe* (Theatr Clwyd); *Deathtrap* (Salisbury Playhouse); *Around the World in 80 Days* (West End/Simon Friend Entertainment); *Peter Pan: The Never Ending Story Arena Tour* (Music Hall, Belgium); *The Mentalists* (Old Vic/West End); *Brave New World* (Royal & Derngate/Theatre Consortium); *The Gift*, *Larksong* (New Vic Theatre, Newcastle Under Lyme); *King John* (Royal & Derngate/Shakespeare's Globe); *Way Up Stream* (Chichester Festival Theatre); *The Famous Victories of Henry V*, *Girl Fights* (RSC); *Animals* (Theatre503); *Blasted* (The Other Room); *The Merchant of Venice*, *King Charles III* (Almeida); *Peter Pan* (Polka Theatre); *Kill Johnny Glendenning* (Royal Lyceum, Edinburgh); *The James Plays* (National Theatre of Scotland/Edinburgh International Festival/National Theatre); *Garw* (Theatr Bara Caws); *Bakersfield Mist*, *Mojo* (West End); *Y Negesydd* (Theatr Genedlaethol Cymru); *Dunsinane* (National Theatre of Scotland/RSC).

Opera includes: *Lucia Di Lammermoor* (Royal Opera House); *Wildman of the West Indies*, *Jason* (English Touring Opera).

Film includes: *Heretiks*, *Genesis*, *Arthur and Merlin*, *Howl*, *The Seasoning House*, *City Slacker*, *Cheerful Weather for the Wedding*, *Deviation*, *Ill Manors*.

RC-Annie Ltd, established in 2005 by Rachel Bown-Williams and Ruth Cooper-Brown, is the UK's leading Dramatic Violence Company.

Support Us

The Tricycle is committed to bringing unheard voices into the mainstream while presenting the world through a variety of lenses.

The support we receive from charitable trusts, corporate partners and individual donors is more important than ever; please join us at this exciting time in the Tricycle's history.

With your support we can continue to:

* *Create world-class theatre, like our critically acclaimed production of* Red Velvet *and Olivier award-winning production* Handbagged.

* *Deliver over 22,000 Creative Learning experiences annually for young people in Brent and beyond to inspire a diverse new generation of theatre-makers and audiences.*

* *Transform the Tricycle into a welcoming space, with a more flexible, accessible and sustainable building in which to see and make theatre.*

Become a Member

Members play a vital role in securing the Tricycle's future by enabling us to present outstanding theatre and empower young people through the arts in the local community. In recognition of their contribution, members receive benefits across stage and screen that include access to priority booking, invitations to exclusive events and discounts on tickets.

Membership starts from £125 a year.

If you wish to discuss our membership levels further please contact the Development Department:

020 7625 0132
development@tricycle.co.uk.

Thank you

We are hugely grateful to our supporters, whose support has contributed to the success of the Artistic and Creative Learning work we produce and provide.

Public Funding

Trusts and Foundations

BackstageTrust

AN ROINN GNÓTHAÍ EACHTRACHA AGUS TRÁDÁLA NA hÉIREANN
DEPARTMENT OF FOREIGN AFFAIRS AND TRADE OF IRELAND

The 29th May 1961 Charitable Trust

Anya Evans Jones Foundation

BBC Children in Need

D'Oyly Carte Charitable Trust

Ernest Cook Trust

Esmée Fairbairn Foundation

Garfield Weston Foundation

Harold Hyam Wingate Foundation

Irish Youth Foundation

J Paul Getty Jnr Charitable Trust

John Lyon's Charity

The Leche Trust

London Schools Excellence Fund

Marie-Louise von Motesiczky Charitable Trust

Network Stadium Housing Association

Pears Family Foundation

The Reso Charitable Trust

Sir Siegmund Warburg's Voluntary Settlement

The Topinambour Trust

Vanderbilt Family Foundation

The Wolfson Foundation

Individuals and Corporate Partners

You can make a gift through your company.
Corporate partnerships offer an opportunity for
businesses and their employees to become part
of the Tricycle Theatre's vision for the future
and receive recognition for their contribution
in bespoke packages.

If you wish to discuss corporate giving further
please contact the Development Department
on 020 7625 0132 or development@tricycle.co.uk

Creative Learning

Young People

The Tricycle has always been known for its work with young people. Since becoming Artistic Director, I have made this central to our mission. For me it is vital that we offer inspirational opportunities that improve the lives of young people. Whether as audiences, writers, performers or producers of new work at the theatre, young people are at the Tricycle's heart.

Indhu

Our Projects

Our work in the local community reaches out to marginalised young people. We work in mainstream and special needs education, with young asylum seekers and refugees and with children in some of Brent's – and the UK's – most deprived areas. The Tricycle helps give all these young people a voice, and the confidence to articulate it.

Tricycle Young Company

Tricycle Young Company offers 11–25 year olds the chance to make high-quality theatre productions; developing skills, confidence and professionalism through work with high-calibre artists.

We are now recruiting for September term. If you're a young actor, producer, or designer interested in taking part please email us at getinvolved@tricycle.co.uk

---

StoryLab

Plays for children, invented by children

The Tricycle's literacy programme for primary schools will run again in 2017 and we're starting to recruit schools.

Participating primary school children will visit the top secret Story Lab at the Tricycle and will be set the challenge: to invent a story so brilliant and so original that storytelling will never be the same again! Their stories will be adapted for the stage and presented in a production in our newly refurbished venue.

If your school is interested in taking part please contact us: jenny.batt@tricycle.co.uk or 020 7625 0134.

For the Tricycle

Artistic Director
Indhu Rubasingham

Executive Producer
Bridget Kalloushi

Head of Production
Shaz McGee

Resident Director
Jennifer Bakst

Marketing Director
Felix Mussell

Marketing Manager
Dawn James

Marketing Officer
Ben Carruthers

Marketing Intern
Nina Primeraki

Development Manager
Katie Wellington

Development Officer
Katherine Ronayne

Creative Learning Director
Liam Shea

**Creative Learning Manager
Young People**
Shereen Phillips

**Creative Learning Manager
Schools and Pathways**
Jenny Batt

Young Company Director
Tom Bowtell

Finance Manager
Paul Canova

Finance Officer
Joe Feehely

Finance Assistant
Elinor Jones

Admin Assistant (Part Time)
Claudia Lander-Duke

Cinema Programmer
John Morgan-Tamosunas

Projectionist
Michael Rose

Relief Projectionist
S R Gobin

Archivist (Voluntary)
Anne Greig

Press Representation
Kate Morley PR

FRONT OF HOUSE

Operations Manager
James Foran

Bar Manager/ House Manager
Owen Sampson

**Operations Officer/
House Manager**
Yoan Segot

**Staffing Manager/
House Manager**
Paul Carstairs

Relief House Managers
Andy Orme
Tara Stroud

Box Office Manager
Kate Roden

Assistant Box Office Manager
Becky Bentley

Box Office Supervisors
Sophie Taylor
Gethin Lewis
Clare Eales-White

Front of House Team

Niall Bishop
Simona Bitmaté
Miles Brown
Aaron Craven-Grew
Helen Crawshaw
Jane Crawshaw
Siobhan Connelly
Clare Eales-White
Jeremy Fowler
Siris Gallinat
Mary Guerin
Rasfan Haval
Katherine Hearst
Steve Hines
Caitlin Hoskins
Chris Hughes
Sonia Jalaly
Felicity Jolly
Daniel Klemens
Zoe Lambrakis
Gethin Lewis
David Noble
Alex Pardey
Jessica Preddy
Maria Pullicino
Heather Ralph
Kal Sabir
David Stroud
Tara Stroud
Sophie Taylor
Patricia Teixeira
Luke Thomas
Alex Williams
Rosy Wilson

Cleaners

Theresa Desmond
Dominic O'Connor
Joslette Williamson
Hua Hua Ye

Tricycle Maintenance
Zeddy

Board of Directors

Baz Bamigboye
Nicholas Basden
Fiona Calnan
Kay Ellen Consolver
Barbara Harrison
Philip Himberg
Jenny Jules
Judy Lever
Jonathan Levy (Chair)
Jeremy Lewison
Anneke Mendelsohn
Philippe Sands QC
Barrie Tankel
Lady Simone Warner

Development Committee

Lesley Adams
Nadhim Ahmed
Baz Bamigboye
Katie Cannon
Kay Ellen Consolver
Sally Doganis
Grant Jones
Mairead Keohane
Judy Lever
Jonathan Levy
Jeremy Lewison
Anneke Mendelsohn (Chair)
Andree Molyneux
Michael Sandler
Christine Scholes
Caroline Schuck
Geraldine Sharpe-Newton

Capital Appeal Committee

Nicholas Basden
Kay Ellen Consolver
Ginny Greenwood
Mairead Keohane
Judy Lever
Jonathan Levy
Jeremy Lewison (Chair)
Anneke Mendelsohn
Michael Sandler

Creative Associates

Lolita Chakrabarti
Adrian Lester
Rosa Maggiora
Lynn Nottage
Tom Piper

**Brent Council
Representatives**

Cllr Muhammed Butt
Cllr John Duffy
Cllr James Denselow

Accountants
Jon Catty and Company

Insurance Brokers
Robertson Taylor W & P
Longreach

The Invisible Hand

It is not from the benevolence of the butcher, the brewer or the baker, that we expect our dinner, but from their regard to their own self-interest. We address ourselves, not to their humanity but to their self-love . . .

Adam Smith, *The Wealth of Nations*

The Invisible Hand had its world premiere as a one-act play on 7 March 2012, at The Repertory Theater of St Louis, St Louis, Missouri (Steven Woolf, Artistic Director). It was directed by Seth Gordon; the set design was by Scott Neale; the costume design was by Lou Bird; the lighting design was by Ann Wrightson; the sound design was by Rusty Wandall; and the stage manager was Champe Leary. The cast was as follows:

Nick	John Hickok
Dar	Ahmed Hassan
Bashir	Bhavesh Patel
James *and* **Guard**	Michael James Reed

The two-act version of *The Invisible Hand* had its New York premiere on 19 November 2014 at New York Theatre Workshop (Jim Nicola, Artistic Director). It was directed by Ken Rus Schmoll; the set design was by Riccardo Hernandez; the costume design was by ESOSA; the lighting design was by Tyler Micoleau; the sound design was by Leah Gelpe; and the stage manager was Megan Schwarz Dickert. The cast was as follows:

Dar	Jameal Ali
Nick	Justin Kirk
Bashir	Usman Ally
Imam Saleem	Darlush Kashani

Characters

Dar, *early twenties*
Nick Bright, *thirties*
Bashir, *mid- to late-twenties*
Imam Saleem, *forties/fifties*

Setting

Somewhere in Pakistan, in the very near future.

The play should be performed with an intermission between
Acts One and Two.

Act One

Scene One

A holding room. Spare. In disrepair. A table center stage. Two chairs. Along the far-left wall, a small cot. And above it, a window near the ceiling. Covered in bars.

There's a door stage right.

Sitting at the table is **Nick Bright**. *Intelligent and vital.*

Across from him is **Dar** – *early twenties, a rural Pakistani who speaks English with a thick accent. He wears a Kalashnikov over his shoulder.*

Dar *is leaning over* **Nick**'s *handcuffed hands. It may take us a moment to realize:*

Dar *is cutting* **Nick**'s *fingernails.*

We hear male voices offstage talking in a foreign language – voices to which **Dar** *appears to be listening.*

Nick   How's your mother, Dar?

Dar   Good. Good.

Nick   That's good.

Dar *smiles, nervously.*

Goes back to cutting.

Nick   So she's not too sick?

Dar   What?

Nick   Your mother. She's not too sick.

Dar   She sick, Mr Nick. She sick. (*Beat.*) But she happy see her son.

Nick   That's good you went to see her, Dar.

Dar *forces a nervous smile, checking over his shoulder as the voices diminish.*

He stops. Listening.

We hear the faint sound of a door closing. Then silence.

Dar *gets up and goes to the door stage right – listening.*

Then crosses to the window upstage center – listening.

In the distance, we hear a car engine start up. Then drive off.

Dar *returns to the table. He rests the gun against the chair. He hands* **Nick** *the nail-cutter as he pulls a key and undoes one of the cuffs.*

Dar   They go. You can cut. I know you don't like I cut for you.

Nick   Thank you, Dar.

The shift is palpable. **Dar** *is clearly more at ease.*

Dar   I not go my mother, Mr Nick. (*Explaining, off* **Nick***'s confusion.*) I not go see my mother. I had plan. I not tell you.

Nick   You had a plan?

Dar   Before I not tell you.

Now I tell you.

You remember my cousin, he have farm? Potato farm?

Nick   Changez, right?

Dar (*smiling warmly*)   You remember.

Nick   Of course I remember, Dar.

Dar   Ramzaan coming. Prices going up and up.

Nick   Like they do every year.

Dar   Changez tell me good crop in Jhelum. Very good year for him.

Nick   I remember.

Dar   Changez is good man, Mr Nick. People like him. He have respect.

Nick   Right.

Dar   I tell him what you tell me. Sell me all potato, all farmer he has friends. Give for me lowest price. I sell potato high price when Ramzaan come.

I tell him, we all share money, together.

Nick   And?

Dar (*nodding*)   He talk to them. They don't sell potato to other. They give me. (*Quietly.*) I tell here, I go my mother.

But I not go my mother.

I get trucks . . .

Nick   . . . Trucks?

Dar   Three trucks. Drive potato from Jhelum to Multan market, highest price.

Nick   How did you get trucks?

Dar   I pay.

Nick   With what?

Dar   Potato. I had so many! (*Laughs.*) After three days, potato gone. (*Beat.*) Seven. Five.

Nick   Seven, five . . . what?

Dar   Dollar.

Nick   Seventy-five dollars.

Dar   I make.

Nick   You're kidding?

Dar   I change from rupee to dollar. Like you told me, Change all your saving to dollar, Dar. More . . . (*Speaking Punjabi.*) pucka.

Nick   Stable.

Dar (*repeating*)   Stable.

Nick   Dar, this is wonderful news.

Dar   A lot of money for me. (*Beat.*) Thank you for give me help.

Nick *smiles, moved. They share a moment.*

We hear sounds in the hall.

Nick *quickly takes a seat.*

Dar *nervously takes the nail-cutter, as* **Nick** *locks the cuff back on to his wrist.*

Just as . . .

We hear the lock of the stage right door opening.

Enter **Bashir** *– mid- to late-twenties, sinewy and intense. A human barracuda.*

Both **Dar** *and* **Nick** *made visibly nervous by his sudden appearance.* **Dar** *stands. A sign of respect.*

Bashir *speaks with a working-class English accent.*

Bashir   Mr Bright?

Nick   Bashir.

Bashir   Been a while.

Three weeks, innit? (*Off* **Nick**'s *silence.*) How've you been?

Nick   Fine.

Bashir   No complaints?

Wouldn't want to be hearing anything about how you'd been mistreated or some such . . .

Want to make sure everything's up to your standards, then.

Nick's *further silence.*

Bashir   Dar taking good care of you?

Nick   Dar is fine.

Bashir   He's a bit of arse-licker, in't he?

But gets the job done sooner or later.

Whatever job that may be . . . (*Patting* **Dar** *on the back.*) I mean he's a good lad.

Takes care of you.

Takes care of his mum.

He looks over and notices that a water pitcher on the table is empty.

What's this? Pitcher's empty? What if Mr Bright needs a drink? What's he gonna do then? Dar?

Dar   I'll get more water.

Bashir   You gonna do that?

Dar   Yes.

Bashir   When?

Nick   It's okay. I'm not thirsty.

Bashir   Well, see, it's the principle now, isn't it?

Dar   You want me to do it now?

Bashir   Yes, I think I do. I think I want you to do it now.

As **Dar** *approaches,* **Bashir** *suddenly strikes him. Viciously. And then again.*

Bashir   Maybe you should go back to taking care of old ladies, you fucking dog!

Nick   He didn't mean it.

Bashir *turns on* **Nick**. *Just as vicious.*

Bashir   Who asked you to open your fucking gob?!

Hmm?!

Did I?!

Nick *looks down. Avoiding eye contact.*

Bashir   That's right. Let's have a little respect around here. (*Snickering.*) I'm guessing it's not going to come as a surprise to you then that our little piss-ant here did not visit his mum this week. Innit?

Nick *shrugs. Not making eye contact.*

Bashir   You didn't know that?

Really?

You had no idea he was out gallivantin' through Multan flogging potatoes?

No idea at all?

Or how 'bout this: That he walked into a Citibank bank two days ago –

You heard of that, right?

Citibank?

Nick   You know I have.

Bashir   That's right. I do. I may know a few things more too. Get ready for it:

Dar here walks into a Citibank the other day and opens an account, that's got interest. Interest.

You and your fucking interest eating up the world like cancer. You been teaching him about cancer then?

Nick   I don't know what you're talking about.

Bashir (*screaming*)   You're a liar!

Nick *looks away.*

Long silence.

Bashir   Citibank's gone cold – you better hope they're getting your ransom together . . . or else –

Nick   What?

Bashir Let's just say, there might be something to be gained turning you into a political prisoner.

Nick I have no importance.

Bashir Man working with the Minister of Water and Energy? Bilal Ansoor? On taking water away from the people?

Nick That's not what I was –

Bashir The fuck it's not!

Nick I've always thought the country's too unstable to privatize water.

Bashir You told Ansoor that?

Nick I've told you. I told him. And I told my boss, a dozen times if I told him once.

Bashir Your boss at Citibank.

Nick Yeah.

Bashir Carey Martin.

Nick Yes.

Bashir I think you're full of shit. (*Shifting.*) Wealthy American looting our country. Taking water from the people. Who knows? Might be some advantage in giving you to Lashkar, innit?

Nick Lashkar?

Bashir Blokes made the video of that journalist. Daniel Pearl.

Nick Right.

Bashir Got his head cut off.

Beat.

You know your wife sent another one of those videos. Julie.

Nick She did –

Bashir   She keeps it together this time. I have to say, I was impressed. She's really a bit of a bird, in't she? Cute kid, too. His hair all messed up, snot coming out his nose . . .

Beat.

Nick   I didn't do anything. I didn't do anything to you! It wasn't even supposed to be me in that car. You thought it was my boss. You don't want me.

Bashir   A bit of bad luck – and not just yours to be honest.

Beat.

He turns to **Dar**.

Bashir (*in Punjabi*)   Bastard!

He grabs **Dar** *by the arm. And pulls him to his feet. Dragging him to the door . . .*

Dar *looks back for a last lingering look at* **Nick** *before* **Bashir** *shoves him out.* **Bashir** *follows.*

Alone, **Nick** *gets up. Pacing.*

When he sees something on the ground.

Reaches down and picks it up.

The nail-cutter.

Nick *holds it in his fingers.*

Lights out.

Scene Two

Three days later. The same room. The cot is further stage left than it was in the last scene.

Nick *and* **Bashir**. **Nick** *is handcuffed.*

Intermittently, through this scene and others, we will hear a recurring distant mechanical buzz. Very faint. Coming in and out.

*The noise will not be referred to – or explained – until Scene Five, by
which point the audience should have become acclimatized to it, unaware.*

There is an iPhone before **Nick**. *Playing. We hear a woman's voice.
The video his wife has made to plead for his life:*

Video   Nick is a good man. He cares about others. He
volunteers on the weekends at a soup kitchen, feeding the
poor. He has a young son, Kaden, who adores him. Please let
my husband go. I've learned that Islam is about mercy and
forgiveness –

Bashir *grabs the iPhone. Stops the video.*

Bashir   Then she goes on and on about Islam, like she's got
a fucking clue.

Silence.

Nick   So they were negotiating?

Bashir   They were. (*Beat.*) No longer.

Nick   I told you it was too much. You didn't believe –

Bashir   That's not it.

Nick   I don't know how many times I've told you –

Bashir   Would you just shut it for a change? (*Beat.*) Imam
Saleem got put on some list. Last week. Your State Department.
The bank can't negotiate. She can't negotiate. It's against
your laws.

Nick   List?

Bashir   Of terrorist groups. (*He snickers.*) Imam Saleem's not
a terrorist. Fucking irony? The Taliban? They don't like us
any more than they like you.

Nick   Right.

Bashir   Imam Saleem's a visionary. He's doing what you
people always promise but never do. He took over the orange
groves to the river. Put people to work. Running the schools,

the hospital in these parts. Money for everything's gotta come from somewhere. You've been robbing us blind for sixty years. We're just taking back what's ours.

Nick   *I* haven't been robbing you –

Bashir (*over*)   Know what was in the paper the other day? Your bank made four billion dollars in three months. Where'd you think all that money came from?

Nick   That has nothing to do with me.

Bashir   Your boss was the big man, Carey Martin, but it has nothing to do with you –

Nick (*cutting in*)   He's not the big man.

Bashir   Ask him for the money yourself? Least he can do, for taking his place.

Nick   I doubt he's got ten million dollars lying around – and even if he did –

Bashir   If he's got bugger all, why's he in the paper all the time?

Nick   He's in the Pakistani papers. Nobody knows who he is outside Pakistan. He's just a banker.

Bashir   And Daniel Pearl was just a journalist.

Beat.

Nick   Cutting off my head is not going to accomplish anything.

Bashir   See, it's not us'd be cutting it off. We don't go in for that sort of thing. That's why we'd be giving you to Lashkar. (*Off a thought, wryly.*) Always wondered about it, though. What's the part of you that – I mean your head's rolling around on the ground, thinking . . . but what's happening to the other part of you? What would it be like being in both places at the same time? (*Beat.*) When you find out, will you tell me?

Long pause.

Nick   We can work something out.

Bashir   Like what?

Nick   I've already told you. I can come up with two and half, maybe three . . .

Bashir   Your ransom's not three. It's ten.

Nick   That's insane! For God's sake, three million you can get is better than ten you can't.

Bashir   I'm actually not sure it is. To be honest. Lashkar's been breathing down our necks. Coming in across the river. Shaking us down for cash. Who knows? Maybe we tell 'em you're a Jew, and you buy us some real peace for once.

Nick   But I'm not Jewish.

Bashir   They're idiots. They won't know the difference.

Nick   I'm not circumcised.

Bashir   Isn't anything can't be taken care of.

Pause.

Nick   God, Bashir. Don't be stupid.

Bashir   Excuse me?

Nick   You've got something of value. Don't piss it away.

Bashir   You got some fucking nerve, don't you? (*Approaching.*) You're the one's yapping that you're not worth sod all –

Nick (*coming in*)   – That's right. To them. To my company. Not worth a penny. Not now. Not after you people kidnapped me. In fact? To them? I'm actually a liability.

But that doesn't mean . . .

Bashir   What?

Nick   That I'm not still worth something . . . to you. Just because you can't get what you want one way, doesn't mean you can't get it another.

Beat.

Bashir   I'm listening.

Nick   Just a month ago, I had a meeting with emerging markets at UBS.

Bashir   What's that?

Nick   Union Bank of Switzerland.

Bashir   Right.

Nick   Their operation is ten times bigger here in Pakistan than Citibank. I was actually in talks to leave Citibank and go to UBS. They were going to pay me a lot more money.

Bashir   How much?

Nick   Seven figures.

Bashir   For what? Showing greedy Pakistanis like Bilal Ansoor how to rob their own people?

Nick   For my understanding of the marketplace. The market climate here in Pakistan. Hell, Carey Martin is an idiot. I've been doing his job for three years. I'm worth a lot more to you alive than dead.

Beat.

Bashir   How'd you work that out?

Nick   I – uh – engineered a trade . . . that cleared the Gaznoor Group twenty million dollars.

Bashir   You mean the Gaznoor family? Richest family in Punjab?

Nick   Gaznoor Group is their holding company.

Beat.

Bashir   How'd you make 'em twenty million?

Nick   Trading wheat.

Bashir   Wheat . . . You're talking about the food shortage.

Nick   No. This was the spring before.

Bashir   That's when the food shortage actually began. Not this spring. Last spring. People buying and selling, fucking up the wheat supply.

Nick   You want to talk about how I made the Gaznoors twenty million dollars or not?

Beat. **Bashir** *finally nods.*

Nick   I recognized a systemic difference in the prices of wheat in Faisalabad and Multan. It was pretty drastic. Nothing to do with agriculture, just an abnormality in the distribution. Once I understood it, I was able to take advantage.

Bashir   How?

Nick   I created an instrument that made it easier for people in Multan to buy wheat in Faisalabad.

Bashir   An instrument?

Nick   A future.

Bashir   Future. Fuckin' hell. Heard of that.

Pause.

Nick   Where are you from?

Bashir   What does that have to do with anything?

Nick   Your accent.

Bashir   You know you've tried that before . . .

That shit's not gonna work on me. I know all about that stupid class they give you when come work in Pakistan: make friends with your captor, get him to see you're a human being.

Nick I wasn't trying to make –

Bashir You really think I'm an idiot, don't you?

Nick I don't think you're an –

Bashir I'm not an idiot. And you best not be insulting my intelligence like that. For your information . . . I had three offers on my UCAS.

Nick UCAS?

Bashir You're not so clever after all, are you, Mr *Bright*? You know about Hounslow?

Nick I don't.

Bashir Well, then, *you're* the ignorant fucker, aren't you? (*Beat.*) You ever take the Tube from Heathrow Airport?

Nick Yes.

Bashir You went right by my house. Had a view of the tracks from my bedroom. If I'd known you were passing by, would have thrown something at your train, you fuck. See, I don't like you. I'll never like you. You're a heartless greedy bastard. And I think the likes a' you are better off dead. You got that?

Nick I got it.

Bashir So what the fuck is a future?

Nick It's a contract to buy something. Or sell something. In the future. If sugar is cheap right now because of – I don't know – over-production in Brazil, you can say, I'd like to keep buying a month from now, six months from now, at today's price. (*Off* **Bashir***'s interest.*) If you do, if you lock in that price, you've bought a future. If the price of sugar goes back up, then it's worth something. You can sell it to make money.

Bashir What if the price goes down?

Nick You can make money a different way if that happens.

Bashir   You can?

Nick   Absolutely. It's called shorting.

Bashir   Right.

Pause.

Nick   There are opportunities.

Bashir   Twenty million.

Nick   Give or take.

Bashir   Wheat.

Nick   Potatoes.

Bashir   A way for people in the south to buy from the north . . .

In the future . . .

Nick   And then we sat back and watched the money roll in.

Bashir *nods.*

With a thought.

Lights out.

Scene Three

Two days later. The same room.

Nick *and* **Bashir**. *And* **Imam Saleem**. *In a white shawl and shalwar. Regal. With charisma to burn.*

He is articulate, but speaks with a pronounced Pakistani accent.

Imam Saleem   When I started out in the world as a young man, it was as a journalist. Writing for the newspaper in Bahawalpur. South of Lahore.

Nick   *Bahawalpur Times?*

Imam Saleem   You know it?

Nick I do. I've spent some time there.

Imam Saleem That was home. Where I was raised. Where my family is from. I knew the place. I knew the people. I wrote local news. Stories I hoped would make some difference.

A village's entire year's wheat crop lost in a fire. A new technique for digging wells that made it easier for farmers to irrigate their fields . . .

I wrote a lot about farmers . . .

A child born to a sharecropper's family who had a remarkable ability in maths. Truly remarkable. That article was a success. Someone with the power to do something read it. That young boy got a scholarship to study in London.

Nick Was that Bashir?

Bashir I told you I was *born* in London. Not Bahawalpur, stupid.

Imam Saleem It was not Bashir. Though it could have been. He's like a son to me now. A very brilliant young man. Despite the occasional lapse. Your kidnapping, for example.

Nick Right.

Imam Saleem The one thing I couldn't write about, the one thing that really mattered, was corruption. (*Beat.*) There is a road from eastern Bahawalpur to the outlying villages. A road some fifty, a hundred thousand people depend on. Unusable.

Pockmarked with potholes the size of a city bus.

Nick Nangni Road.

Imam Saleem Right. Every year in local council Nangni Road was at the top of the list. Every year it was brought up in Parliament. Every year it was voted on, approved, paid for. For ten years. But the road has never been fixed.

Nick No, it hasn't.

Imam Saleem   I wrote an article. Told the story of where that money might have been going. My editor killed it. Of course, I was fired. Lectured about how I should know better. Two days later, my father was coming home from work. Three men ambushed him. They beat him to the ground with chains. He was left on the side of the road. They told him: 'Tell your son not to worry about Nangni Road. It's fine just the way it is.'

Nick   Jesus . . .

Imam Saleem   For three days, he survived. Long enough to berate me for my foolishness. (*Pause.*) You see, we are prisoners of a corrupt country that is our own making. But don't pretend you don't participate. You do. Of course you do. That's your job. That was Mr Carey Martin's job. To grease the wheels, to rape and plunder our nation. (*Off* **Nick**'*s silence.*) I commend you for not objecting, Mr. Bright. (*Pause.*) It was a very long path from that young man whose father was killed because of him to the person you see before you today. A long journey, but a straight one. A clean line. A clean line of outrage. (*Pause.*) Are you following me, Mr Bright?

Nick   I believe so.

Imam Saleem   What am I telling you?

Nick   That you kidnapped me . . . so you can fix roads.

Pause.

Imam Saleem (*wry*)   Exactly. (*Beat.*) When Bashir came to me with your idea, I was skeptical. But he made a passionate case. We have a growing annual budget. If he had a deeper understanding of the financial side of things, that would be very helpful, indeed. So . . .

If I am inclined to take you up on the offer, it will be as much for the sake of his education as for the prospect of the full ransom being paid.

Nick   Well, you'll have to reduce your expectations on the ransom, sir. Three million I can get. I can turn it into five. Feel confident about that. Ten? That's not likely.

Bashir   But that's what you said.

Nick   That's not exactly what I said.

Bashir   It bloody well is!

Nick   I didn't –

Bashir (*cutting him off, angry*)   – You said you made the Gaznoors twenty million. You could do the same for us.

Nick   I wasn't locked up, being held in some room.

Bashir   Fucking hell . . .

Imam Saleem (*in Punjabi*)   Bashir. Calm down. (*To* **Nick**, *in English.*) You don't have to humor him, Mr Bright.

Beat.

Nick (*to* **Imam Saleem**)   You have to give me a realistic goal. Or I won't be effective. Give me something I can really work toward.

Bashir   Fucking hell . . .

Imam Saleem (*to* **Bashir**, *in Punjabi*)   Calm down. (*Beat.*) Twenty million?

Nick   I had infrastructure, support.

Imam Saleem   You will have Bashir to assist you.

Nick   I had a team. A half-dozen people.

Imam Saleem   How long did it take? (*Off* **Nick**'s *silence.*) How long?

Nick   Four months.

Imam Saleem   Twenty million in four months. So ten million in two.

Nick   Sir . . .

Imam Saleem   But, of course, there were six of you . . .

And now you are only two . . .

Nick   One. I'm only one. *They* were professionals.

Imam Saleem   Fine. The work of two months but you have to carry the labor of six. Two times six. Twelve months. You work to make your full ransom. If you are diligent, well-behaved, but haven't made the full ten million in one year's time, we will revisit the terms of your captivity.

Nick   A year?

Imam Saleem   Mr Bright. Enjoy the mercy I am showing you.

Nick   I don't think you understand what you're asking.

Imam Saleem   I think you are the one who does not understand.

Long pause.

Nick   I'm going to need things. Access to information. To markets.

Bashir   I've been looking into that.

Imam Saleem   Very diligently, you will be happy to hear.

Bashir   Can all be arranged. Through a good laptop.

Imam Saleem   You won't be allowed within a meter of any computer.

Nick   No more handcuffs.

Imam Saleem   That is at Bashir's discretion.

Nick   Not acceptable. My hands need to be free. I need to be reading, making notes. I cannot work with these.

Bashir (*coming in with the key*)   You get any fucking ideas?
They'll be back on your wrists right quick.

Beat.

Imam Saleem (*to* **Nick**)   You are certain you can get the
three million?

Nick   There's a way. Through my personal accounts in
Grand Cayman.

Pause.

Imam Saleem   Then it's settled. We keep you alive. Bashir
learns what he can. You make your ransom. We let you go.

Beat.

Nick   What's my assurance?

Imam Saleem   My word is your assurance.

Nick   Your word?

What happens when you don't like me any more? Or when
you start having problems with Lashkar again?

Imam Saleem   Lashkar?

Nick   Bashir told me –

Imam Saleem (*cutting him off, to* **Bashir**)   We are not
Lashkar. We have nothing to do with Lashkar. I don't want
to hear that name. They call themselves Muslims. They're
animals. (*Turning to* **Nick**.) When I was sick, very sick some
years ago, I spent some time with my brother in Trenton,
New Jersey. Not far from where you went to school.
Princeton, right? (*Off* **Nick***'s surprise.*) Don't be so surprised.
We *should* know some things about you by now.

So much struck me about your country. The poverty. Which
I did not expect. And the fat people. But what I found truly
amazing, was the lawyers. At the hospital, more lawyers than
doctors. But not only there. *Nothing* happens in your country

without a lawyer. That's what it means to be American, isn't it? Nobody's word means anything.

Beat.

Lights out.

Scene Four

That night.

The room is dark except for the sharp streak of silver moonlight coming through the single barred window.

Nick *lies on the cot, still.*

Beat. He sits up in bed.

Quietly, **Nick** *heads for the door downstage right and – getting there – kneels, his ear to the lock.*

He listens for a long beat. We may or may not hear the faint sound of snoring wafting through the door from the hall on the other side.

Nick *looks satisfied as he stands and now heads for the window upstage center. On his way, he quietly scoops up a chair from its place at the table center stage.*

Placing the chair silently against the far wall, he stands on it and peers out the window.

Nothing there. Only the faint sounds of insects at night.

Now **Nick** *heads for his cot, carefully pushing it out of the way to expose the wall and make room for himself . . .*

As he pulls out the nail-cutter . . .

. . . kneels and begins picking away at mortar between the bricks in the wall behind where the cot stood.

We listen to the soft scratching sounds, and watch him work.

Lights out.

Scene Five

Three days later.

The same room.

Now center stage taken up by two tables. Both covered with newspapers, financial magazines, papers written on, etc.

At one table, **Nick** *sits buried in the paper. And in printouts.*

At the other table, **Bashir** *is in the process of fiddling with a laptop. Loading software and installing.*

Throughout the scene, we should barely register the intermittent distant buzz mentioned earlier.

Nick   What about Jalalabad Concrete?

Bashir   I didn't ask.

Nick   But he was sure about Srinagar Industries?

Bashir   Imam said that's for sure.

Nick   But see, Jalalabad has the same history of price spikes whenever there's good political news for President Randani.

Bashir   So it's prolly his. Wouldn't be surprised. Mr Thirty Percent.

Nick   Ten. Don't they call him Mr Ten Percent?

Bashir   That was before he was President. Now? He takes as much as he wants, the greedy midget. Chota. That's what they call him.

Nick   Chota?

Bashir   Yeah. Means small. Which he is. Prolly more ways than one.

Nick   You know I've met him a few times.

Bashir   Randani?

Nick   It's true. He's smaller than you'd expect.

Bashir Don't say it to his face. The man's a fuckin' sadist.

Nick I've heard the rumors.

Bashir My uncle? Owned a petrol pump in Islamabad.
One day, a black limousine stops for petrol. Randani gets out.
Looks around. Bastard goes inside, very nice, very charming.
Shakes my uncle's hand. Takes off. Two days later, some of
his men show up. Turns out Mr Asif Randani would like to
buy the station. And not for the going market rate, if you get
what I mean. My uncle didn't want to sell. But he did. After
he lost two fingernails on his right hand. You Americans have
been keeping him in power.

Beat.

Nick Well, says here President Randani's day is coming.

Bashir So what if it does?

Nick If Randani is indicted, his net worth is going to take a
major hit.

Bashir And?

Nick The companies he owns will, too. That's information
we can use to make money. Trading's about having an edge.
Knowing something, understanding something that others
haven't figured out yet.

Bashir An edge?

Nick Yeah.

Bashir But you're reading about that in the newspaper . . .

Nick What's your point?

Bashir So you're not the only one who knows it . . .

Nick Well, yeah, but . . .

Bashir So what's your edge?

Beat.

Nick *ignores the question. Noting the distant buzzing sound.*

Nick   What's that sound? I always hear that . . .

Bashir   Drones. Americans keeping their eye on Lashkar . . .

Fuckin' nightmare with those things flying around.
Everybody's always running for cover. You never know what
they're going to hit.

Nick   I haven't heard any explosions.

Bashir   Then you're not listening.

As **Bashir** *continues to work on the computer* . . .

Nick   So you're saying the Imam confirmed Srinagar as a
definite yes.

Bashir   And Buttee Holding Company. Don't forget that
one.

Nick   Right. Buttee.

Bashir   And Asmaan Textile Group. Imam said President
Randani owns that too.

Nick *shifts attention back to his list.*

Nick   Okay.

So with Jalalabad, that makes four companies. Let's start with
that . . .

Are you logged into the exchange yet?

Bashir   Still waiting on that approval to go through.
Waiting on calls and something or other.

Nick   Puts.

Bashir   That's right. What are those?

Nick   Remember options to buy?

Bashir   Yeah.

Nick   Puts are options to sell.

Bashir (*perplexed*)   Okay . . .

Nick   Look, just type those companies names and the words 'options chains' into Google.

Bashir   I don't get it.

Nick   Get what?

Bashir   Why'd you be buying that stuff if you reckon they're gonna go down in price?

Nick   We're going to short those companies. Bet against them.

Bashir   Okay . . .

Nick   It's how you make money off a stock that's dropping.

Bashir   How do you – I mean . . . how's it work?

Nick   We buy puts.

Bashir   Right.

Nick   When the price drops. The value of the puts rises.

Bashir   Doesn't make any sense.

Nick   It does. Just not to you. Not right now. If you don't mind, I'd like to get to work. Which means I need you to get online and pull up –

Bashir   I'm not your dog.

Nick   Excuse me.

Bashir   I'm not your slave.

Beat.

Nick   We have a job to do. Two days ago I asked you to get Lexis-Nexis. Where are you on that?

Bashir   Looking into it.

Nick   That's what you said yesterday. What's there to look into?

Bashir   It's complicated.

Nick   You know you got real excited about the money I made for the Gaznoors. But I can't even get the tools I need to start working –

Bashir   I've gotta make sure it's not some tracking software or something.

Nick   Lexis-Nexis is not tracking software. This is what I'm talking about. I don't have time for this –

Bashir   I've got a question? Your job's to explain it to me. Mr Big Shot.

Nick   My job's to make money. You'll learn whatever you learn by watching. That's how I learned.

Bashir   You look down on me.

Nick   Excuse me?

Bashir   You think I don't know that?

Nick   I don't know what you're –

Bashir   Because of what I'm doing. Here. At least that's what you think. But that's not it. Not even. 'Cause it wouldn't be any different I was back in London driving around in some black beemer in my Dolce Gabbanas, chasing white pussy. You'd be looking down on me then, too, just in a different way.

Nick   I think you're calling me a racist.

Bashir   I think you're right. (*Beat.*) Beaten up at the bus stop and 'Paki go home'. Stopped and searched. Stopped and searched. Fucking embarrassed when my mum would take me to the shopping center. Fucking embarrassed of my own mother. That's what you people did to me.

Nick   I didn't do –

Bashir   The fuck you didn't. Both ways. That's how you lot want it. Better than everyone else *and* we should feel as good about it as you do.

Nick   Uh-huh.

Bashir   My father? Spent his whole life being stepped on, spit on by you people. Playing the servant during the day, tyrant with us all at night. But you know what? He let you do it to him. He's the one left Pakistan in the first place. The whole generation of them, looking to leave what they shoulda been working to make better. This country's gone to shit because people like my father wanted something better for themselves. Selfish fucking bastards.

Silence. **Bashir** *is inhabited by a profound and personal rage.* **Nick** *can't help but notice.*

Nick   This? Is not helpful.

Bashir   Of course not. Nothing you like hearing, so isn't helpful.

Nick   You done?

Bashir   No, I'm not. Something else I was good at in school? History. Though you probably don't believe that, neither.

Nick   I never said –

Bashir   I remember this course we had about European history. The Spanish Civil War. All these young men from different countries running off to give their lives to fight the dictator, Franco. That's what I'm doing. Giving up a soft life in the West to fight for something meaningful. Fucking irony. D'you know Ronald Reagan had the Taliban to the White House when he was president? Called 'em the moral equivalent of your founding fathers.

Nick   I doubt it.

Bashir   He did. I'll show you. It's on YouTube.

Nick   I'd really rather you'd pull up the options chains for the companies we're talking about.

Beat.

Bashir   For what? Your shit idea everyone else already knows about?

Nick   You have a better one?

Bashir   An edge? Right?

Nick   Yeah?

That's what you're looking for? Information no one else's got?

Nick   You have it?

Pause.

Bashir   I know this bloke.

Nick   Bloke.

Bashir   He's an Arsenal fan.

Nick   Sorry?

Bashir   Football. Soccer. He's got access to a satellite dish. We get together for the games. (*Beat.*) He's in with Lashkar. (*Beat.*) Match the other day. We got to talking about the Minister of Water and Energy, your best mate –

Nick   Bilal Ansoor –

Bashir   That's it.

Nick   He's not my best mate.

Bashir   Told me Lashkar's planning to take him out.

Nick   When?

Bashir   The way he was talking about it ... Sounded like soon. Turns out Imam Saleem's not the only one who thinks privatising water is not in the people's interest.

Beat.

Nick   Can you find out more?

Bashir   Yeah.

Nick   I'll get to work on a new list.

Lights out.

Scene Six

Two days later.

Bashir *sits at the table, the laptop open. Eager.*

Nick *paces behind him. Agitated.*

Nick What time is it?

Bashir Ten past three.

Nick Why hasn't it hit the news yet?

Bashi I don't know.

Nick You said two o'clock.

Bashir That's what he told me.

Bashir *refreshes the screen. And again.*

Nick Still nothing?

Bashir No.

Nick Can you call him?

Bashir No.

Nick Text him. Text him.

Bashir No.

Nick You have the trading screen open?

Bashir Yes.

Nick All five companies listed?

Bashir Look for yourself.

Nick *peers in over **Bashir**'s shoulder.*

Nick Good. (*Scanning.*)

Jaan Subsidiaries.

Paani Filter Technologies.

First Wave Ltd.

Gwadar De-Sal.

What about Kaghan Pure? Where's that?

Bashir   Right in front of you. 'KPOXX'.

Nick   Oh, right.

He steps away. Pacing.

So those are the water concerns I know Bilal Ansoor had major ownership stakes in. I don't know if they're all exposed the same way. And he's probably got more. But that should get us somewhere.

Bashir   So what are you worried about?

Nick   Are you kidding me? It's a fucking huge position. Two and a half million on a bunch of crappy options.

Bashir   What's the risk? If nothing happens –

Nick *(coming in)*   Cost of the transaction? On a two and a half million dollar position? Significant. And that's if nothing happens. If for some reason, prices don't drop, but rise? We lose serious money.

Beat.

Nick   You know what? Fuck this. Let's get out. Go to the sell screeen –

Bashir *(perking up)*   Okay. There it is. *Pakistan Times*. 'Breaking news. Suicide bombing in Karachi. Omni Hotel.' Yep, yep. 'At least fifty injured.'

Nick   What about Ansoor? Did they get him?

Bashir   Doesn't say.

Nick   Shit.

Bashir   What now?

Nick   Just wait. See what happens.

Bashir   Nothing.

Nick   Just keep waiting.

Pause.

Those are real-time quotes, right?

Bashir   You know they are.

Nick   Actually, I don't. I didn't set it up.

Bashir   They're real-time. (*Suddenly.*) Right, here we go. Jaan and Paani down. Jaan three, four and a quarter. Paani down two and half. Two. Two and a half. Four. Wow. Christ, Nick. Just like that. Went down seven.

Nick   Okay, it's not a lot, but they're moving together. Just keep watching.

Bashir   Kaghan, First Wave not moving. But . . . Gwadar De-Sal . . . down – wait a second – thirteen rupees.

Nick   They must have gotten Ansoor.

Bashir   First Wave starting to move down. Four rupees. Six. Nine and half. Seventeen. Kaghan moving, too.

Nick   What's the rest of the market doing? The other window.

Bashir (*clicking over*)   Not much.

Nick   How's volume?

Bashir   Where's that.

Nick   The last column.

Bashir   That one?

Nick (*approaching the computer*)   Right. Good.

They're pouring in. Buyers are coming in.

Bashir   Kaghan down fifteen to two twenty-five. Paani down twenty-four! Jaan down forty-three rupees. Jesus. They're moving, Nick! They're moving!

Nick   Yeah, it's picking up now.

Bashir (*excited*)   What do I do?

Nick   Nothing. Just wait. Stay calm. Making money can get intoxicating. You have to stay sober. Bad things happen when you're not thinking straight.

Bashir   Everything down. Dropping.

Nick   The rest of the market?

Bashir   Steady. (*Suddenly.*) Here's the first official report. (*Reading.*) 'Among the dead is controversial Water Minister Bilal Ansoor. Ansoor's death will spell some uncertainty for the large-scale water privatization that has been under way in parts of Sindh Province.'

Nick   How many people were killed?

Bashir (*reading*)   'Forty-five confirmed dead. Seventy-eight wounded.

'Ansoor was in attendance at the wedding of his eldest daughter.'

Nick   It was a fucking wedding?

Bashir (*reading*)   Ansoor's wife, the well-known film actress Fiza Qureshi, was also reported killed.

Nick (*alarmed, quietly*)   Holy shit.

*He looks over **Bashir**'s shoulder. Conflicted. Thinking.*

*As **Bashir** continues . . .*

Bashir   Kaghan dropping through the floor.

Down another fifty-three.

Gwadar down . . .

Thirty-seven . . . Forty-three . . .

Paani dropping . . .

Seventeen and a half . . .

Finally:

Nick (*decisive*)   Sell.

Bashir   What?

Nick   Start selling.

Bashir   But the prices are falling.

Nick   Bashir. Just do it.

Bashir   Why? We're still making money.

Nick   Volume's dropping. It's gonna turn. Get out.

Bashir   It's not turning.

Nick   Bashir –

Bashir   Kaghan down another forty-one to two thousand eighty –

Nick   I understand the situation here –

Bashir   Gwadar's still moving, too –

Nick   And I understand that I'm in charge right now. So just do as you're told. Sell. (*Off the screen.*) Look. See? First Wave. Isn't moving. (*Beat.*) Put in the order to sell. (*Beat.*) Do it!

Bashir *finally relents.*

Bashir (*confused*)   Sell at market?

Nick (*irritated*)   No. At the current ask.

They'll wait to fill the orders and skim. We're selling a lot of contracts. Pennies matter.

Bashir *types orders in . . .*

Nick *watching* . . .

Nick   Goddamnit, Bashir! Not like that. Put the number in there.

Look, just let me do it.

Bashir   Get back. Now. You are not touching the computer. (*Back to typing.*) In there?

Nick   Yes.

Bashir *keeps typing in the orders.*

Nick *watches.*

Bashir   Kaghan sold. 2,500 contracts at 2,051. (*Typing, beat.*) First Wave position . . . closed at 174 rupees. (*Typing, beat.*) Paani closed at 671. (*Typing, beat.*) Gwadar closed at 156. (*Typing, beat.*) Jaan Subsidiaries . . . (*Waiting.*) now closed at 495 and half rupees.

Nick   Proceeds?

Bashir   One hundred and fifty-one million six hundred thousand forty-three rupees.

Nick (*calculating*)   . . . So we made roughly seven hundred thousand dollars.

Pause.

Bashir *continues to watch the screen.*

Bashir   Prices are still dropping. (*Silence.*) Kaghan down another seventeen rupees.

Nick   Bashir –

Bashir   First Wave down another twelve . . .

Nick   Bashir, look at me.

Bulls make money. Bears make money. Pigs get slaughtered.

Bashir   What the fuck is that?

Nick   What they say on Wall Street.

Being a bull or a bear means you have a disciplined philosophy about the market. You stick to it? You get rich. Greed is what loses you money.

Bashir   You think leaving cash on the table is going to make you feel better about your best friend and his wife blown to shit?

Nick   He wasn't my best friend.

Bashir   She give you a good blow-job?

Nick   This is not about me wanting to feel better.

Bashir   Bollocks. You're fucking soft. The whole lot of you. Can't even fight a war any more.

Nick   That's enough.

Bashir   Send a bunch of drones around – 'cause you don't have the stomach to face death yourself. Yours or anyone else's.

Nick   I said that's enough!

Pause.

Bashir (*back at the screen*)   Still dropping . . . (*Beat.*) Gwadar's down to one thirty-nine.

Bashir*'s mood shifts as he sees something on the screen. Tapping* . . .

Wait a second . . . (*Clicking.*) I don't believe it . . . The exchange . . . has stopped trading.

Nick   What are you talking about?

Bashir (*reading the screen*)   'Trading on selected securities suspended . . .'

Nick (*reading the screen*)   'Until further notice.' Unbelievable.

Bashir (*reading*)   All trading halted for fourteen companies. (*Searching.*) Kaghan, First Wave, Jaan, Paani, Gwadar . . .

Yeah, they're all on the list.

Nick   You sure we're out of those positions?

Bashir *types again. Waits . . .*

Bashir   Yes.

Nick   Six minutes. Bilal Ansoor's powerful friends started losing money. And ten minutes is how long it takes them to shut down trading.

Bashir   Pakistan.

Nick   You'd be surprised. It doesn't just happen here.

Awkward silence.

Don't forget to convert the proceeds to dollars.

Bashir   Now?

Nick   Yes.

Bashir *starts typing into the computer.*

Nick   The rupee is one political crisis away from insolvency. Downward pressure on the rupee means we make money just by keeping dollars.

Bashir (*off the computer screen*)   Okay. Rupees converted.

Nick   Okay. Well, we're done for the day.

Long pause.

Bashir   Well done. You got us out.

Nick   Yeah. Well. I couldn't have predicted that.

Bashir   What a disaster if we'd been left with that stuff . . .

Nick   Not necessarily. I mean they have to start trading again at some point. (*Beat.*) But I wouldn't want to have to sleep on that.

Long pause.

Bashir *goes to* **Nick**'s *cot. Takes a seat.*

Bashir   I'm sorry.

Nick   For what? It's fine.

Bashir   No, it's not. I was being a wanker. It's not appropriate. I saw the numbers dropping. I was getting greedy.

Beat.

Nick   Like I said, pigs get slaughtered.

Bashir   Not in Pakistan, mate. (*Lying down.*) You're right about making money. It really is a bit like being pissed, innit?

Nick   Pissed?

Bashir   You know. Shit-faced. Drunk.

Nick   Right.

Pause. **Nick** *doesn't ask the obvious question.*

Finally . . .

Um – Bashir, you know, I don't have a lot of things of my own at this point and . . . Well . . . Do you mind letting me have my own bed . . . ?

Bashir (*realizing*)   Right.

Nick   Thanks.

Bashir *gets up. And goes to the table. Where he sits.*

Bashir   You sleeping okay on that thing?

Nick   Fine.

Bashir   Maybe we should get you another one.

Nick   I'm fine, Bashir.

Bashir   Something more comfy.

Nick   I'm used to it now. I like it.

Bashir *nods.*

Silence.

Bashir   I know you don't get it, but sometimes the revolution is violent. And sometimes the peace can only come after the violence.

Beat.

Nicks *nods. Not affirming. Not denying.*

Another long pause.

Nick   Good work, today.

Bashir *nods.*

Blackout.

Scene Seven

Night.

Nick *is alone.*

He stands on the chair, looking out the window. Taking in a scene we cannot see.

Yapping dogs in the distance.

After a long beat, he quietly steps off the chair and returns it to the table. Pulls the cot out quietly and resumes the work of digging discreetly at the wall with the nail-cutter . . .

Lights out.

Scene Eight

The following day.

The same room.

Bashir *and* **Nick***. At the tables.* **Nick** *explaining.* **Bashir** *listening and responding. Computer open before him.*

Nick   The most important thing about money, Bashir, is that people don't like losing it. People, companies, governments.

So they're always looking for safe places to put it. For seventy years, the safest place has been the US dollar.

Bashir   But why the dollar?

Beat.

Nick   Okay . . . The Second World War. Europeans had destroyed each other. Destabilized the world economy.

Bashir   Okay . . .

Nick   The world's currency rates were a mess. So the decision was made to get everyone on gold. To stabilize things. But that only worked if someone could *guarantee* the price of gold. The US came in and did that. If France wanted money for their gold? They came to America. Germany, England? Same thing. Effectively, we became the world's bank. Which meant the dollar became the world's safest currency.

It was called the Bretton Woods system.

Bashir   The what system?

Nick   Bretton Woods. It's the town in New Hampshire where they came up with this idea.

Bashir   Bretton Woods . . . (*As he pulls an iPhone.*) Thought I recognized that . . . (*Pulling something up and reading.*) Bretton Woods and the Changing Role of the Central Bank. By Nick Ernest Bright.

Bashir *shows* **Nick** *the screen.*

Bashir   That's yours, right?

Nick   That's my senior thesis.

Bashir   It's what came up on the third page when I typed your name into Lexis-Nexis.

Nick   You downloaded my Princeton senior thesis on to your iPhone . . .

Bashir   Didn't know what else to do with it.

He pulls the phone, then returns it to his pocket. Gets up from the table.

Nick *returns to perusing papers on the table. Working through some numbers.*

Bashir *has gotten to the window, where he stands listening. The by-now familiar distant buzzing of flying drones.*

And then ever so faintly, beneath the buzzing – what could be an explosion.

Bashir   You hear that?

Nick   What?

Bashir   Listen.

More buzzing. And another distant explosion.

Nick   Yeah.

Bashir   Drone attack.

Nick   How far is that?

Bashir   Other side of the river. Ever since Lashkar hit Bilal Ansoor, they've been feeling the pain. (*Pause, turning back to* **Nick**.) So I've been wondering . . .

Nick   Yeah . . .

Bashir   If people have it in their interest for a stock to go down, can't they just do stuff to make it go down?

Nick   Theoretically, yes. But the market is huge. A single player can't usually affect –

Bashir   What's to stop them from getting together and making the price drop?

Nick   Laws. There's laws against that. (*Beat.*) I mean, look. When I was working at a hedge fund, would people leak word about a stock, sow a rumor, buy a huge position just to get the market to move?

Bashir   That's what I'm talking about.

Nick   Right, but even then – even if they do – it's a short window. The market catches on. So you can do that. And banks on Wall Street do . . .

Bashir   It's what we did with Bilal Ansoor.

Nick (*distracted by the papers*)   I mean . . .

Bashir   Isn't it?

Nick   We didn't *kill* him.

Bashir   Don't worry. No blood on your hands. I'm just saying: We had the information.

Nick   And see how short that window was? It was just a few minutes before the market started correcting itself.

Bashir *turns his attention back out the window.*

As **Nick** *turns back to the statements:*

Nick   Wait. Are these from last night?

Bashir   Yes.

Nick   Did you look at these?

Bashir   Not yet.

Nick   We're missing money.

Bashir   Did that go through?

Nick   Did what go through?

Bashir   Expenses.

Nick   Expenses? Are you serious?

Bashir   For your toilet paper.

Nick   You people can't –

Bashir   It's not you people. It's Imam Saleem. He needed it.

Nick   For what?

Bashir   Vaccines.

Nick   That's the capital base. I need that money to trade.

Bashir   A stolen shipment from one of those pharmaceutical companies. $150,000 is a small price to pay.

Nick   There's $400,000 missing. Not $150.

Bashir   What? (*Going over to check.*) He said it would be $150.

Nick   That's what they all say.

Bashir   What are you talking about?

Nick   Wake up.

Bashir   I'm sure there's a reason it was more.

Nick   The reason's as old as the fucking hills . . .

Bashir   Four hundred thousand . . .

Nick   The money is actually worth more than that. The purchasing power. The trading power that it gives us.(*Beat, exasperated.*) Fucking ridiculous.

Bashir   Stop being such a bitch.

Nick   I'm the bitch?

Bashir   Little fucking whining bitch.

Nick   I'm the one bitching and moaning 24/7 about how everybody looks down on me, and everyone thinks they're so much better than me . . . and the whole load of whiny crap coming out of you and your fucking Imam? Who probably didn't even buy any fucking vaccines.

Bashir   Fuck you.

Nick   No. Fuck you. And fuck your sleazebag Saleem.

Bashir   You forget where you are, Mr Bigshot?

Nick   No, I didn't fucking forget! I didn't forget my wife. Or my three-year-old son. Or some stupid idea I had to make you fuckers money to save my life. My wife's hair is probably falling out of her fucking head right now? Kaden? He has no idea what's going on. And I have no idea what Julie is telling him. But whatever she's saying? I know he knows something's wrong. And he's goddamn right there is.

You know what else I didn't forget? Your promise to let me go. I know how much your Imam hates lawyers, but when I hear about four hundred thousand dollars missing from our trading account, I'll tell you, I wish I had a fucking lawyer.

Long pause.

Bashir (*troubled*)   I don't know why he wouldn't tell me.

Nick (*off* **Bashir**'s *seed of doubt*)   I've been around money a long time. And I've seen a lot of things. But there's one thing that doesn't change. What money does to people. When you get a taste, you want more.

Bashir *recognizing the truth of this from his own experience.*

Tense silence.

Blackout.

Scene Nine

The next day.

The same room.

Imam Saleem. Bashir. Nick. *And . . .*

Dar. *From the beginning of the play. Looking meek, cowered.*

All look on solemnly as:

Imam Saleem *peruses the folders and papers on the table. Taking things in.*

He finally speaks . . .

Imam Saleem (*warmly*)   We were very impressed with the results of this week's work. Almost eight hundred thousand dollars, hmm?

Nick   Closer to $850,000 actually, after today's session.

Imam Saleem   Well done.

Nick   Well, I'm working very hard, Bashir and I are working very hard, to build the capital base –

Imam Saleem   I understand.

Nick   Do you? I mean, because my capital base is my only leverage in the market. If you dilute my cash position . . .

Imam Saleem   The future health of the local children comes before your *cash position*.

Nick   Sir, that's not actually our agreement. If you want to remove funds from the trading account, I think we should be having a conversation about lowering the ransom amount.

Imam Saleem   Mr Bright . . .

Nick   Sir, please. Just hear me out. Three and a third to one. That's what you want me to make. Take three million turn it into ten. At that ratio, four hundred thousand dollars is actually worth a million and a half. Which would mean that the more realistic ransom number, now, after the withdrawal, is eight and a half million.

Imam Saleem   I see.

Nick   Do you?

Imam Saleem (*continuing*)   Can I call you Nick, or is it Nicholas?

Nick   Whatever you want.

Pause.

Imam Saleem   Just yesterday, Nick . . . I found myself in a conversation with you. My wife thought I was losing my mind, when she found me talking to myself in the evening.

Nick   Okay.

Imam Saleem   Humor me, Nick. (*Beat.*) I found myself wondering if perhaps you were the sort of person who thought religion is the opiate of the people?

Nick   That's Marx.

Imam Saleem   I know who it is.

Nick   I don't know why you thought I was the sort of person who –

Imam Saleem (*suddenly*)   So you don't believe religion keeps the people sedated, unthinking, accepting of the conditions that oppress them?

Beat.

Nick   I . . . think lots of things can do that.

Imam Saleem   Very good answer. Very politic.

Nick   I'm not being politic.

Imam Saleem   I'm not sure I believe you. (*Pause.*) Do you believe in God?

Nick   I'm not sure what relevance . . .

Imam Saleem   Humor me. Please.

Nick   I guess . . . yes, I believe in God.

Imam Saleem   And what is your God called?

Nick   He doesn't have a name, exactly. He's a . . .

Imam Saleem   Feeling . . . ?

Nick   Yeah. That's right. He's a feeling.

Imam Saleem   And what do you do for this feeling?

Nick   What do I do for it?

Imam Saleem   What are you prepared to do? Do you *feel* any sense of obligation to this feeling?

Nick   Not really. It's just there.

Imam Saleem   It's there for you, to feel at your convenience . . . would you say?

Nick   I'd just say it's there. Convenient or not.

Pause.

Imam Saleem   So let me ask you this: what, in your opinion, can motivate people to do the most extraordinary things? Can money do that?

Nick   I don't know.

Imam Saleem   What do you think? I want to know. Is money at the root of the great fulfilled lives in human history?

Nick   I guess I would say no. It's not.

Imam Saleem   Right. Exactly right. (*To* **Dar**, *gesturing.*) As I told you.

Dar *steps over and starts cuffing* **Nick***'s hands behind his back.*

Bashir (*with concern*)   Imam sahib?

Nick   Wait, what's going on?

Imam Saleem (*continuing*)   You see, I believe that *money* is the opiate of the people, not religion. Money is what puts people to sleep when it comes to the moral dimension of life.

And the only tonic, the only remedy for this slumbering sickness of money . . . Do you know what it is?

Nick   What?

Imam Saleem   Sacrifice.

He pulls out a gun. Turns to **Dar**.

Imam Saleem (*in Punjabi*)   Take it.

Bashir   What are you doing?

Dar *steps forward, meekly. Hesitant. Finally takes the gun.*

Nick   Did I say something wrong?

Imam Saleem *gestures for* **Dar** *to point it at* **Nick**.

Dar *obeys. But with difficulty.*

Imam Saleem   One thing that has always made me very angry about Americans is the way they confuse money with righteousness. Being rich does not give you moral superiority, Nick Bright . . .

Bashir   We made an agreement.

Nick   If I did something wrong, I'm sorry.

Bashir   He's making us money –

Imam Saleem (*continuing*)   Three thousand of your people die on one day and it gives you license to kill hundreds of thousands of our people . . .

Nick   We can leave it at ten million. It's fine.

Bashir   Imam Sahib.

Imam Saleem   And to feel so good about it. You are murdering hypocrites! And for that, Nick Bright, you deserve to die!

Nick   For God's sake. Listen to me.

Bashir   What are you doing?

Imam Saleem (*ignoring* **Bashir**, *to* **Dar**)   Kill him.

Nick   Dar. Please, no. Don't kill me.

Bashir *approaches* **Dar**, **Imam Saleem** . . .

Bashir   Why are you doing this?

Imam Saleem (*to* **Dar**, *in Punjabi*)   Kill him, I said.

Bashir   No. You're not doing that. (*Stepping in front of the gun.*) Not now. No. That's not what you promised.

Imam Saleem *strikes* **Bashir**.

Imam Saleem   I changed my mind. (*Beat.*) Move – I said, move!

Nick   What I made for you two days ago? I can do it again. I can. Just don't kill me!

Imam Saleem (*to* **Dar**)   Do it.

Nick   Please! No! Dar! Don't!

A dark stain spreads across **Nick***'s pants as he wets himself.*

Dar *pulls the trigger.*

Click. Empty.

Pulls again. Empty again.

Nick   Oh God. Oh God. Oh God.

Dar*'s shoulders collapse. Broken by the test.*

Nick *reels from the surge of adrenaline terror.*

Imam Saleem *steps over to* **Dar***, approving. Takes the gun. With a kiss to* **Dar***'s forehead.*

Imam Saleem (*in Punjabi*)   Good job, son. (*To* **Dar***, pointing at* **Nick.**) Free him.

He turns to **Bashir.**

Bashir *can't meet the* **Imam Saleem***'s gaze.*

Imam Saleem *looks knowingly at his charge. Having learned all he wanted from this display.*

Imam Saleem (*to* **Nick**)   We are expecting great things from you. Just don't ever forget where you are. And who you are.

(*To* **Dar***, in Punjabi.*) Go.

Dar *leaves.* **Imam Saleem** *turns to* **Bashir.**

Imam Saleem   I'll see you at juma prayers.

Bashir *nods.*

Imam Saleem *exits.*

Nick *looks over at* **Bashir***. In shock.*

Beat.

Scene Ten

Night.

The same room.

Nick *at the wall, the cot pulled away from the area he has been working on.*

He is at work. Pulling bricks quietly. One by one. A hole he has created, just large enough for him to wiggle through.

A sound outside the door.

He stops.

Listens.

Nothing.

Then back to work. Pulling the last few bricks.

With a final look around, he begins to crawl through.

The stage is empty.

Silence that lasts a long moment.

Finally, the aggressive barking of dogs in the distance.

Lights out.

Act Two

Scene Eleven

Five weeks later.

The tables and walls are covered with the result of **Nick** *and* **Bashir***'s work in the market:*

Stock charts, stochastics, Black-Sholes models.

As lights come up, we find **Nick** *standing at a wall, with a ruler to one of the charts, making calculations and then marking the chart with a pencil.*

He leans back, with a thought.

He turns to head for the table . . . (We won't notice until now that his ankles are attached by a long chain to a bolt in the floor. And that he is now walking with a pronounced limp.)

At the table, he shuffles through some papers, makes another note.

We hear a door unlocking.

Bashir *enters, a bag dangling from his shoulders.*

Bashir   Morning, Nick.

Nick   Bashir.

Bashir *comes to the table, starts unpacking his bag at the table.*

All part of what seems like a routine . . .

Nick   Bashir . . .

Bashir   What?

Nick *(indicating his feet)*   Can we get these . . .

Bashir   Yeah. Sorry. *(Toward offstage.)* Dar!

Dar *appears at the door.*

Bashir *(in Punjabi)*   Unchain him.

Dar *does as he's told, more reserved around* **Nick** *than he was at the opening of the play.*

Nick   Is this really necessary? I mean, my leg –

Bashir   Enough with the leg, already. I don't know what you expect when you punch a fucking hole in my wall and –

Nick   It hurts. I'm serious. As far as I know, after what those fucking dogs did to me I'll end up with gangrene.

Bashir   Doctor said you were fine.

Nick   I'm not. And this thing only makes the pain worse.

Bashir   Get used to it. Because the only time it's coming off is when I'm in the room with you.

Nick   Look, I know I made a mistake. Okay? I know. And I'm paying for it. Why this on top of everything –

Bashir   It's not coming off.

Nick   C'mon, you would have done the same in my shoes.

Bashir   Wouldn'ta done the same at all. Because I wouldn't of gotten caught. (*Beat.*) Anyway, that chain's your best mate, Nick. You should be snuggling with it. It's only reason you're not dead.

Nick   Yeah, right.

Bashir   It is. Imam Saleem was ready to –

Nick   What? He was ready to do what?

Beat.

Bashir   You thought that thing with Dar and the gun was bad? You should have seen him when he found out you'd tried to escape.

Nick   Yeah, and then a week later, he shows up here with the hospital books and wants my advice on balancing the budget. He's no idiot. He knows he's got a good thing going. Plus, we're making him too much money.

Beat.

Bashir   That's not what we're doing. Making *him* money. We're making it for the people.

Nick   That's not my point.

Bashir *(irritated)*   You done about the chain? 'Cause if you don't shut up about it, I'm gonna put another one on you.

Nick *is quiet.*

Bashir *pulls a folder from his bag.*

Bashir   Finally found those balance sheets you wanted.

Nick   Just set them down there.

Bashir   Took a bit of doing, actually . . . Deep web . . .

Nick   If it was easy, everybody would be doing it.

Bashir   I'm going to have a cuppa. You?

Nick   Yeah. Fine.

Bashir *(to **Dar**, in Punjabi)*   Tea. For me, and the white guy.

Dar *nods. Exits.*

Bashir *yawns as he keeps unpacking.*

Nick   Up late again?

Bashir   Was up till four a.m. doing financials on those ideas you floated. Sixty- and ninety-day moving averages. Little ruler analysis, like you showed me.

He tosses another folder across the table.

Can't get enough of this stuff. And can't stop thinking about it. Been making me wish I'd gone to uni to do economics . . .

Nick   Quickest way to kill a passion. *(Beat, making notes on his pad.)* Listen, when you get that thing up, I'm gonna need you to hop on and look into some of these trades I want to try. And I want to check on that Communion Capital Dividend.

Bashir   Oh, that hit.

Nick   It did?

Bashir   Last night.

Nick   I didn't think it would hit until the twenty-first.

Bashir   Today's the twenty-second.

Nick   It is? (*Beat.*) Shit.

Bashir   What?

Nick   It's my son's birthday.

Bashir   Seriously?

Nick   Would you . . . Could I message out to him?

Bashir   No. (*Beat.*) Communion Capital. Two hundred forty thousand and change. Puts us up over five and a quarter million.

Eighty per cent in eight weeks.

Nick   Wow. Anybody knew about that return, I'd make the cover of the *Wall Street Journal* . . . (*Beat.*) Did you ever talk to your guy at Lashkar?

Bashir   Not yet.

Nick   If he has information, Bashir . . .

Bashir   I know.

Nick   Anything we can use . . .

Bashir   Haven't seen him.

Nick   When you do . . .

Bashir   You'll be the first to know.

Nick   Because we're in a position to really capitalize here.

Bashir *takes up* **Nick***'s note pad.*

Bashir   What are these?

Nick   Quick, rupee-related trades. In and out.

Bashir   You love the rupee.

Nick   Love to hate it.

Bashir   Buying puts?

Nick   Someone is going to make a killing shorting the rupee. One more major political crisis in this country . . .

Bashir (*mimicking, American accent*)   'And the rupee is bust, Bashir'

Nick   It's true.

Just as . . .

Dar *appears at the door. With tea service.*

Bashir   Suppose if the Pakistanis had any sense in their brains, they'd be tying the rupee to a basket.

Nick   A what?

Bashir   Basket of currencies.

Nick (*surprised*)   You're right.

Bashir   Don't be so surprised. Got the idea from you.

Nick   I don't remember talking about –

Bashir (*cutting him off*)   From your thesis. (*Pulling his iPhone.*) Been reading it finally. After doing that ruler analysis, I knocked off a couple of chapters. Burning the candle, like I said. (*Off his iPhone again.*) Just started that part on currency being king. Fucking central bankers? Those are the *real* power brokers. And I mean that whole Bretton Woods thing was fucking brilliant. Perfect Trojan horse.

Nick   Trojan horse?

Bashir   The Greeks. They built this wooden horse. Left it outside the city of Troy.

Nick   I know what the Trojan horse is.

Bashir   You just asked me.

Nick   What's the connection with Bretton Woods?

Bashir   The whole getting-everyone-back-on-gold thing. Seemed like a good idea. Everybody let it right in. Little did they know, out would creep the dollar. Take over the world.

Nick   Interesting. I mean, all Bretton Woods *actually* did was lay a framework –

Bashir   Right. For the US dollar to be at the center –

Nick   To be a support.

Bashir   The center.

Nick   I get that you hate America. I hope – for you – at some point you'll outgrow your prejudices.

Because they don't have much to do with reality.

Bashir   Nick. The dollar is a piece of paper. It's not gold.

Nick   What's your point?

Bashir   The US figured out a way to make everyone *think* it was gold. To treat it like gold. I mean all those years the whole world was looking up to you – my parents' generation? They thought America was the greatest place on the planet. Because you made them depend on dollars, and then stuffed 'em down their throats with a smile.

Nick   'Stuffed them down their throats'?

Bashir   Innit? He who controls the currency controls the world. Like I said, I'd no idea it was the blokes running the central banks who're in charge.

Nick   Were we at the top of the food chain? Yes. Did we have more money than everyone else? Yes. And what did we do with it? You needed money to get things done? We gave it to you.

Bashir   In dollars.

Nick   You don't want anything else. It's the only thing that's stable. We spent on military security. We created this thing called the IMF that helped everyone out when they got behind. We created the conditions to make it work. So that we could grow together. Countries that don't trade with each other go to war with one another other. Very few wars have been fought between countries that have McDonald's. Bretton Woods was about cooperation. Growth. Peace.

Bashir   Bollocks.

Nick   Bollocks?

Bashir   You're make it sound like it was a bunch of hippies singing 'Kumbaya' and sucking each others' dicks.

Nick   Bashir . . .

Bashir   It was about taking advantage. That's what it's about. Like the Spanish, back in the day. Going to the New World, telling everyone they were going to bring *Christ* to the *heathens*. What was that all about? Gold, silver, land. Or the English running around – to *civilize the savages*. What were they really doing? Taking tea, rubber. Taking land. And then America's in charge. Bringing growth, cooperation. With Bretton Woods. 'Democracy' with war in Iraq. But what are you really doing?

Nick   Power is what it is.

Some have it. Some don't.

Those who don't, want it.

The best the rest of us can hope for?

That those who have it, will use it well.

For all its faults, America tries to use it well.

Bashir   I suppose that's what you sound like when you've been drinking the Kool-Aid all your life.

Nick   Better in our hands than it would have been in the Germans. Or the Russians. Or than it would be now with the Chinese.

Bashir *considers.*

Nick   I got you there, innit.

Bashir   I'm gonna have to think about that . . .

Nick   You logged into the exchange yet?

Bashir   Doing that now.

Lights out.

Scene Twelve

That night.

Nick *and* **Imam Saleem**.

Nick *has a binder open before him, is going through figures, as* **Imam Saleem** *listens and participates:*

Nick   Look, I just don't think you're doing as well in your wholesale agreements as you could. I don't understand why you're –

Imam Saleem   It includes transportation. Saves me that expense.

Nick   But even with transportation, this deal costs you too much.

Imam Saleem   Transporting the oranges to the nearest market is not easy. The only road takes you through Taliban controlled area and the wholesaler has a relationship with them. His brother is in their leadership.

Nick   Well, then, revisit the labor costs. I mean –

Imam Saleem   Labor?

Nick   The crop hasn't yielded the past two years, but you haven't cut wages.

Imam Saleem   We're barely paying the people enough as it is.

Nick   You're losing money. That's the bottom line. It's not sustainable. I suppose you could keep kidnapping bankers to cover the shortfall . . .

Imam Saleem *doesn't find this particularly funny.*

Nick   But barring that, there must still be another solution. (*Beat.*) Look, when Bashir gets here in the morning, I'll get him to pull up some background on the orange market –

Imam Saleem   No need. This is separate. Keep him focused on the trading.

Nick   It's fine.

Imam Saleem   I said there was no need. (*Off a thought, pulling a letter.*) I meant to show you something else.

Hands him the letter.

Nick *reads. Long beat.*

Nick (*with alarm*)   When did you get this?

Imam Saleem   Three days ago.

Nick   Three days . . .

And you're showing it to me now?

We just spent an hour talking about your orange groves?

Imam Saleem   What's the problem?

Nick (*off the letter*)   Whose name is this? Mulazzam ...

Imam Saleem (*correcting pronunciation*)   Mulazzam. Official registrant.

Nick   Who is Mulazzam?

Beat.

Imam Saleem   The name on the account.

Nick   He's an actual person . . .

Imam Saleem   My wife's cousin.

Nick   What's his profile?

Imam Saleem   Profile?

Nick   Does he attract attention?

Imam Saleem   He's been dead twenty years. (*Beat.*) What's the concern?

Nick   When I was working for the Gaznoors, sir, they got a letter like this, too.

Imam Saleem   The Gaznoors . . .

Nick   Yes. We're nowhere near the filing date. This letter is letting us know we're on somebody's radar. (*Off the letter.*) Zafar Tanweer. Executive, Tax Collectorate. Signed in blue ink. Wants you to know he's on the case. You know this guy?

Imam Saleem   No.

Nick   This is not good. We're going to need to start moving the money.

Imam Saleem   Moving the money?

Nick   This is actually not about the tax. A reminder to file? Two months early? It's a test. They want to know whose money this is. Five and a quarter million dollars sitting around in account registered to a rural hospital. In a dead guy's name. Looks fishy, because it is fishy.

Imam Saleem   I see.

As far as Mr Tanweer knows, it could belong to an MP hiding cash, maybe someone even more dangerous. He is trying to *ascertain* if he's gonna end up with a severed horse's head in his bed should he try to collect. And we need to send him the message that, yes, *you* are a person not to fuck with.

Pause.

What happened with the Gaznoors?

Nick   Nothing. Because I took care of it.

Imam Saleem (*cautioning*)   Nick . . .

Nick   Sir, we need to do what those in power in this country always do with their money. We need to launder it.

Imam Saleem   How?

Nick   It's difficult. The money'll have to be carved up. I'd send it to Dubai, then use hawala brokers to route it back. They'll have to be paid off. Once the money is back in Pakistan, we'll shelter it in illiquid assets.

Imam Saleem   'Illiquid'?

Nick   Real estate. Which you'll need to purchase in someone else's name. Ideally, someone who's alive. All of this needs to take place as quickly as possible.

Imam Saleem   Real estate.

Nick   A house. Land. Commercial building. Something tangible. Something you can borrow against.

Imam Saleem (*off a thought of his own*)   We started repairs on the irrigation system for the orange groves . . .

Nick   So?

Imam Saleem *doesn't reply.* **Nick** *presses:*

Nick   Wait . . .

You were planning to use my trading money again? To do repairs on your irrigation system?

Imam Saleem   Nick.

Nick   When were you going to tell me this? You have me going over your books but you don't tell me the one thing that –

Imam Saleem   Nick.

Nick   I can't fucking believe it. I'm in here busting my ass –

Imam Saleem   Watch your tone.

Nick   Or what?!

Suddenly, **Imam Saleem** *hits* **Nick**. *Hard.*

Imam Saleem   That.

Beat.

Then **Nick** *continues, undeterred.*

Nick   If you don't handle this situation correctly, they won't just come for the tax. They'll liquidate the entire account. They'll take it all.

Imam Saleem   If that happens? You're a dead man.

Nick   Sir . . .

I don't know if you fully understand what I'm up against. You gave me a year to make ten million. This is going to add weeks, months to the process. While this happens, I won't be able to make a cent toward my ransom. Not one single cent.

Imam Saleem   Your point?

Beat.

Nick   You need me. Goes without saying I need you. But you need me too. Let me get a message back to my wife. That's all I'm asking.

Imam Saleem *considers.*

Blackout.

Scene Thirteen

The following morning.

Nick *sits.*

Bashir *stands before him, with an iPhone.*

Bashir   Nothing complicated, Nick.

Nick   I know.

Bashir   Don't try to get any kind of secret message out.

Nick   I'm not an idiot, Bashir.

Bashir   Okay. So . . .

Nick *collects himself. Then looks up at the camera.*

Bashir (*pressing a button*)   It's recording.

Nick (*looking into the camera*)   Hi, guys. It's me . . .

All at once, long-pent up emotions come rising to the surface. He tries to push through . . .

I miss you both . . . so much. Honey, I hope you're okay. Kaden, happy birthday.

Every syllable only drawing more emotion to the surface. Until he can't go on. And breaks down, crying.

Bashir *lowers the camera.*

Looking on.

Finally, **Nick***'s tears run their course. He wipes them away with his shirt. Gets up and moves around, hoping to shake off the emotion.*

Bashir   You want to try again?

Nick   Can we wait?

I don't want my son to see me like this . . .

Bashir   I haven't got all day.

He puts the phone down.

Long pause.

You and the Imam, huh?

Nick   What?

Bashir   You got him to let you get a message out. How'd you do that?

Nick   I asked.

Bashir   That simple, was it?

Nick   Of course it wasn't that simple. Nothing here is.
(*Offhand.*) It was the tax letter.

Beat.

Bashir   What tax letter?

Nick   He didn't tell you about that.

Bashir   No.

Nick   So he didn't tell you about how we won't be able to
trade for weeks while we move the money around?

Bashir   Move it where?

Nick   Or that he was going to pull more funds from the
trading account to repair the irrigation system for the orange
groves?

Bashir   When?

Nick   Maybe pocket a little, or not so little, on the side, like
the last time he pulled money from the account.

Bashir   You're lying.

Nick   Who is this guy? This guy you'd lay your life down
for. You haven't seen your family, in what, five years? For
this guy? Who doesn't tell you shit, even though you're the
one making him all the money?

At which point **Bashir** *has had enough …*

Bashir (*suddenly*)   Fuck you, Nick. And fuck your wife.
I hope some bloke is shagging her as we speak, you cunt.

He goes to the door.

Dar! Dar!

Dar *appears*

Bashir (*in Punjabi*)   Put that chain on him.

Dar *comes over. Starts to do so.*

Nick   Bashir, I'm sorry. Please. I didn't mean . . .

Bashir *leaves.* **Nick** *turns to* **Dar**.

Nick   Fuck. (*To* **Dar**.) Dar. Please. Tell Bashir, I'm sorry. I got carried away . . .

Dar *finishes up and walks out.*

Lights out.

Scene Fourteen

Two days later.

Bashir *and* **Dar** *stand downstage, in the middle of a conversation – an air of intrigue between them.*

Upstage, the only door to the room is open. From which we may hear a few discrete sounds. Humming.

The conversation is partly in Punjabi (italicized).

Dar   *I kept a good distance from the car. He didn't see me or the scooter. They drove around from some time, then went into the city.*

Bashir   And then?

Dar   *I lost him –*

Bashir   *Lost him?* You lost him? How could you lose him? That's the only thing you had to do . . .

Dar   *Just for a little while. There were so many people in the bazaar.* I went back to their car. And I waited.

Bashir   *Then?*

Dar   They came back after a few minutes, got into the car, *and drove to an office.*

Bashir   *They?*

Dar   *He was with his wife.*

Bashir   His wife? He went to pick up his wife?

Dar   *Yes.*

Bashir   From where?

Dar   *I don't know.* But she had a bag of sweets.

Bashir   Sweets?

Dar   Jehan Sweet Shop.

Bashir   What?

Dar   They have very good Gulab Jamun there. Everybody goes for the Gulab Jamun.

Bashir   Okay. I get it.

Dar   *They drove to Murree.*

Bashir   Murree . . .

Dar   *They parked outside a black building.* He went inside.

Bashir   Did he go inside alone?

Dar *nods.*

Dar   *When he came out, it was with a man.*

Bashir   *Who?*

Dar   *I don't know.*

Bashir   *Then what?*

Dar   They went into the car, *and drove to a house.*

Bashir   Do you know whose house it was?

Dar   *Letters in the mailbox said Khurrum Chaudury.*

Bashir   Khurrum Chaudury.

Dar   *They went inside.* And when they came out, she didn't have the bag of sweets.

Bashir   How long were they inside?

Dar   Thirty minutes.

Beat.

Bashir   Who is Khurrum Chaudury? I never heard that name.

Dar   I call Rashid.

Interrupting the conversation –

From offstage, through the open door, we now hear **Nick***'s voice:*

Nick (*offstage*)   I'm finished. Can you unlock me?

Bashir (*to* **Dar**)   *Go take care of him. But wait . . .*

He takes out a thick wad of dollars. Peels off bills. Hands them to **Dar**.

Dar *takes them. Visibly surprised. Grateful.*

Dar   Hundred dollar?

Bashir   And don't forget. Half of it's for you. The other half you give to someone who needs it.

Dar *pockets the note. Walks out.*

Beat.

Finally, **Nick** *enters. Led in by* **Dar**. *One of* **Nick***'s wrists is in a handcuff.*

Nick *uses a key to undo the other cuff.*

He removes them and hands them to **Dar**.

Dar   I call Rashid now. Find out.

Bashir (*in Punjabi*)   *You do that.*

Nick   Find out what?

Bashir   Excuse me?

Nick   I mean . . . Right.

He goes back to the table, sensing something is going on.

He watches **Bashir** *pace and get more and more worked up.*

Nick *is silent.*

As **Bashir** *paces, muttering under his breath.*

Finally:

Nick   Everything okay?

Bashir   Yeah, fine.

Nick   Yeah?

Bashir   Great, actually. Why you asking?

Nick   I mean . . .

Bashir   Just shut up.

Nick   Okay.

Just as **Dar** *returns. Phone to his ear.*

Bashir (*to* **Dar**)   What is it?

Dar   Rashid.

He repeats what he's hearing on the other end of the line. Punjabi in italics.

Dar   *That house is for sale.*

Bashir   The house is for sale?

Dar   *I remember that building the man came out of? It had a real estate office.*

Bashir   Real estate. That must be why he had his wife. They must have been looking at the house.

Dar   With a bag of sweets?

Bashir   I don't fucking know. What's the asking price of the house?

Dar (*into phone, in Punjabi*)   *How much is the house?* (*Beat, to* **Bashir**.) He don't know.

Bashir   Tell him to find out. (*Beat, then calling* **Dar** *back.*) Dar. Wait. Call him back.

Dar (*into phone, in Punjabi*)   *I'll call you back.*

Bashir (*to* **Dar**, *in Punjabi*)   *Chain him up.*

Dar *returns and binds* **Nick**. *As* **Bashir** *begins to collect all the paperwork in the cell.*

Nick   What's going on?

Bashir   I'll be back.

Nick   Wait, what are you doing? We've got work to do.

Bashir   Well, that's actually none of your fucking business, now, is it? (*To* **Dar**, *in Punjabi.*) Get everything.

Dar *and* **Bashir** *finish collecting the room's paperwork.*

Nick   Bashir . . . Bashir . . .

Bashir (*stopping before the door*)   What?

Nick   Don't – uh . . . Don't make your move too soon.

Lights out.

Scene Fifteen

One day later. Night.

Nick *on his cot. Clearly anxious.*

There are sounds outside. Someone approaching.

Then sounds at the door. The lock loudly snapping.

The door opens, and **Imam Saleem** *enters.*

Imam Saleem *shuts the door. Locks it.*

Nick   Imam.

Imam Saleem *comes into the room. Stands and holds* **Nick**'s *gaze for a long moment.*

Nick   Is everything alright?

Imam Saleem   I hope you have a good explanation.

Nick   For what?

Imam Saleem   The money, Nicholas.

Nick   What money?

Imam Saleem   What money? What money do you think?

Nick   The money in the trading account?

Imam Saleem   The trading account is empty.

Nick   What?

Nick *gets up. Winces as he moves his leg. Clearly in more pain than before.*

Imam Saleem   I did not sanction you to move funds.

Nick   I did not move any funds. Are you sure it's empty? Did you check with Bashir . . .

Imam Saleem   If you tell me now, maybe, just maybe, I won't kill you.

Nick   I have no idea −

Imam Saleem   What did Bashir offer you?

Nick   Sir −

Imam Saleem   Freedom? Did he promise you freedom?

Nick   No, no. Nothing −

Imam Saleem   Whatever he told you, you are very stupid to believe. Very stupid. He's gone. (*Approaching.*) I will kill you with my bare hands . . .

Nick   I have no idea what you're talking about −

Imam Saleem   An account in Grand Cayman Island. The money was transferred yesterday. I'm to believe that Bashir moved funds to an account in Grand Cayman by himself?

Without your assistance?

Pause.

Where is he?

Nick   I don't know.

Imam Saleem *is choking* **Nick**. *Finally* **Nick** *coughs up:*

Nick   He was having you followed.

Imam Saleem   What?

Nick   He was . . . having you . . . followed.

Imam Saleem   Followed . . .

Nick   He and Dar, while you were away.

Imam Saleem   Mm-hm.

Nick   Looking at real estate? (*Off* **Imam Saleem**'s *silence.*) I overheard a conversation.

Imam Saleem   With who?

Nick   Don't know On the phone. Didn't get all of it. You were with your wife. Looking at houses. Something about a bag of sweets.

Pause.

Imam Saleem   Behanchod.

Nick   When Bashir heard about the real estate, it made him very angry. Then he left. That was yesterday. It's the last I saw him.

Imam Saleem   If I find out you had *anything* to do with this. You will pay for it.

He moves to the door to exit.

He nods. Despite himself.

Then exits.

Nick *moves to sit. To take weight off his leg. Clearly in pain.*

Blackout.

Scene Sixteen

Three days later.

Nick *alone.*

Clearly unnerved by what we will discover is three days of isolation.

When the lights come up, we find him muttering to himself.

Nick   If they know what they want to do . . . They can do it . . . I mean they can do it, but they have to tell us first . . . Which means you have to get them to tell us, because if they don't tell us . . . But that means you have to talk to them . . . We cut them in . . . They can have a cut. That's the deal we'd make with anyone else. Why not them? . . . But you have to talk to them first . . . If they have something, and if they do, we make it worth their while. We can do that, but not if you don't talk to them . . . Not more than two and half. Two and half per cent of ten million. Or wait. Two and half per cent of eight and a half. Two twelve and a quarter. That's minus fifteen per cent. I know, I know. But we can't get away with thirty. That's a bridge too far. Fifteen, half of thirty. Minus ten is eight and half. Two and a half of eight and a half. Two twelve a quarter. Then you take the other fifteen. One-eighty. Give or take. One-eighty is a good number. Give five if you have to.

Just as we hear . . .

The sounds at the door . . .

Dar *appears.*

Nick   Dar. Thank God. There you are. (*Beat.*) What's going on?

Dar *ignores the question. Goes to the covered metal pail in the corner. Takes it up. There is something pent-up in him.*

Nick   I need toilet paper, Dar.

Dar *exits. Leaving the door open.*

When he returns, it is with the empty pail. Puts it back in its place.

Nick   I need toilet paper.

Dar   I heard it.

Nick   Where's Bashir, Dar? Please just tell me where he is. It's been three days.

Beat. Finally:

Dar   I do not know.

Nick   Where's the Imam?

Dar *moves to exit.*

Nick *stops him:*

Nick   Dar. Please. Don't go.

Dar *stops.*

Nick   Where's the Imam?

Dar *stares blankly back. Not answering.*

Nick   How's your mother, Dar?

Dar (*perplexed*)   My mother?

Nick   She okay? (*Off* **Dar***'s silence.*) Your cousin, Changez?

Must be at the beginning of a new cycle for the potato crop. How's he doing?

Dar   I go now.

Nick   Dar. Please.

Dar   Mr Nick, I look you. You tell Imam one thing. You tell Bashir other thing.

You do not care anything but you.

Nick   You're the same.

Dar   You do not want die. But everybody die. You die. Like everybody.

He glares at **Nick** *for a beat. Hostile.*

Then exits.

Snapping the door lock shut behind him once he's out.

Lights out.

Scene Seventeen

The following day.

Nick *alone. At the table. Trying to occupy himself. However ineffectually.*

Just as we hear –

The door unlocking. **Bashir** *enters. Looking chipper.*

At first, **Nick** *is surprised to see him. Thrown, even.*

Bashir   Morning, Nick.

Nick   Bashir.

Bashir   Fuck. It reeks in here.

Nick   Thank God you're back.

Bashir   Worried about me, were you?

Nick   Well, I had no idea if you were . . .

Bashir   What? If I was what? (*Pause, then suddenly.*) We should get that thing taken off. Your leg and all, right?

Nick   I'd appreciate it.

Bashir   How's it doing?

Nick   Not good. It hurts.

Bashir   Should get a doctor in to see you.

Nick   Yes. That'd be good. Thank you.

Bashir *goes to the door.*

Bashir   Dar! Dar! (*Turns back inside.*) He'll be right here to get that thing off you.

Nick *notices:*

Nick   Where's your computer?

Bashir   Oh, right.

Nick   We need to get back to work . . .

Bashir   About that . . .

Nick   We still have open positions. Those put options contracts on the rupee. I have no idea how those have done.

Bashir   Might not be needing that.

Nick   We may need to get out of them.

Bashir   You might be busy with some other things for the time being . . .

Just as . . .

Dar *appears at the doorway, with* **Imam Saleem**, *beaten, bloodied, bound.*

Bashir   Keeping the Imam a little company, innit? Seeing as you two are so chummy now. Maybe you could give him some more advice on . . . (*Turning to* **Imam Saleem**.) investing in real estate.

Imam Saleem   It was to save the money –

Bashir   Buying a house in your wife's name for a million dollars. *To save the money* –

Imam Saleem   *He* told me to do it.

Nick   I did not.

Imam Saleem   He's lying.

Nick   I told you we had to get the money out first, and then hide it in property. I never told you to buy a house for your fucking wife.

Imam Saleem   You are a cancer. Conniving, malignant cancer.

Bashir *turns to* **Nick**.

Bashir   He isn't wrong about that, is he?

Nick (*pleading*)   Bashir, I did –

Bashir   Save it, Nick. Dar's told me a few things . . .

Imam Saleem   Just securing the funds, like he told me.

Bashir   Like you *just* needed $150,000 for vaccines but you took $400,000. (*To* **Nick**.) You know what I found out? Those vaccines didn't even cost $150,000. It was forty thousand he paid. Pocketed the rest.

Imam Saleem   I didn't pocket –

Bashir   That's the people's money! Not your money! Not your wife's money!

Imam Saleem   You speak for the people now? Hmm? You think anyone will follow you?! You're a child!

Dar *comes over and kicks* **Imam Saleem**.

Bashir *laughs*.

Imam Saleem *moans, coughs*.

Bashir *looks over at* **Nick**.

Nick   Bashir . . . Please. I was just trying to help him move the money. But not so he could –

Bashir   Whatever, Nick.

Both **Dar** *and* **Bashir** *move to exit*.

Before leaving, **Bashir** *pulls out his phone. Snaps a shot of* **Imam Saleem***. Then:*

Bashir (*to* **Dar**)   Let's go.

Both exit. Snapping the lock shut.

Leaving **Nick** *with* **Imam Saleem**, *who continues to moan quietly in pain.*

Lights out.

Scene Eighteen

That night.

Nick *in bed.*

Imam Saleem, *on the floor. Still bound.*

Silence. Until . . .

Nick *turns over, clearly still awake. Locks eyes with* **Imam Saleem**.

Imam Saleem   Do you know Abbottabad, the city? In the north? Where they got Osama Bin Laden.

Nick   Do I know it?

Imam Saleem   Have you been?

Nick   Once.

Imam Saleem   What do you remember about it?

Nick   Not much.

Imam Saleem   Army town. Everywhere you go, soldiers. Did you think it was strange *that* was where Bin Laden was hiding for ten years. (*Off* **Nick***'s silence.*) Before the Americans got him, I'd been hearing rumours that Bin Laden was in Abbottabad. Musharraf was in charge of the country at the time. *General* Pervez Musharraf. And Bin Laden was being kept in a military town.

Nick *turns away. Trying to shut* **Imam Saleem** *out.*

Imam Saleem   The United States had been pouring billions of dollars into Pakistan to find him. For ten years. *Billions*. Would you give up the very reason all of that money is coming into the country? And now that he's dead? Not even half the money is coming in. He was the cash cow. Like you.

Imam Saleem *laughs. And coughs.*

Pause.

Nick   Was Bashir right? Did the vaccines only cost you forty thousand?

Imam Saleem   I told Bashir you played us – each off the other. I told him you took advantage of our ignorance to pit us against one another.

Nick   That's not true.

Imam Saleem   Isn't it? *(Beat.)* There you were, telling me, 'Look for illiquid assets.' She always wanted a house . . . I don't know . . . I always felt guilty . . . And here you were, giving me the permission . . . *(Beat.)* We were sitting in the living room, discussing the offer, sweets on the table. She was so happy. And then I saw it. All at once. How lost I am. Lost to the money.

Long pause.

Nick   Bashir won't kill me. He needs me.

Imam Saleem   You are the cash cow. But Bin Laden's time came, too. *(Beat.)* My father died in my arms, crying like a dog. Fear in his eyes. Disbelief. How could it be happening? How could it be ending? Now?

Just as . . .

We hear something at the door. The lock snapping open.

Dar *comes in, a kerosene lamp in one hand, a gun in the other.*

Uncharacteristically vicious in his demeanor.

Barely acknowledging **Nick**, *he sets the lantern down on the table and goes to* **Imam Saleem**. *Brusquely lifting the ailing man to his feet. Then he drags him out of the room.*

Leaving the door open.

Nick *goes over to the open door to look, getting there just in time to see –*

What we will hear –

Imam Saleem   Allah hu Akbar.

Then a gunshot. And another.

Silence.

Dar *comes back into the room.*

Nick *flinches. Convinced he is next.*

Nick   No, please, don't, Dar . . .

Dar, *heaving from the adrenaline of killing* **Imam Saleem**, *looks over at* **Nick**. *With a chilling, inscrutable expression. By the light of the kerosene lamp, we see:*

Dar's *face and clothes are splattered with blood.*

Dar *takes up the lamp and exits. Locking the door behind him.*

Leaving **Nick** *alone. Heaving . . .*

In his moment of terror, **Nick** *drops to his knees, and a prayer flows out, unbidden:*

Nick   Our Father, who art in heaven, hallowed be thy name; thy kingdom come; thy will be done on earth as it is in heaven . . .

Broken.

Blackout.

Scene Nineteen

Nick *alone. Disheveled. He has been on his own now for three weeks.*

Papers are strewn everywhere.

He sits on the ground. Looking deeply disoriented.

He walks over to the wall. There's a piece of paper on the wall. He stares at it. Pulls the piece of paper, holds it, staring. And then puts it in his mouth.

Just as we begin to hear the very distant sounds of gunfire.

An explosion.

And then more gunfire. The countryside awash in sudden violence.

Nick *arrested, listening.*

Scene Twenty

The same room.

Two days later.

Papers still strewn about.

Bashir *stands, a newspaper folded under his arm, looking at* **Nick**.

Bashir *is arrayed in resplendent robes reminiscent of those we saw on* **Imam Saleem**. *He has a new bearing, a new confidence and charisma.*

We are listening to the continuing sounds of distant gunfire. The sounds of war.

Dar *stands stoically guard, covered in ammunition-filled belts and holding a Kalashnikov.*

Bashir   There is blood in the streets. The city is on fire. Fighting even as far outside as across the river.

Nick   Please. Bashir. Please.

Bashir   What's that?

Nick   I know . . .

Bashir   What do you know, Nick?

Nick   I know you don't owe me –

Bashir   Owe you?

Nick   Let me get back to work. Please. I've been in here by myself for I don't know how long. I can't . . . Any more . . . Let's come to an agreement. Any kind of agreement.

Bashir *approaches. Tosses the paper down on the table before him:*

Nick   What is it?

Bashir   Last Friday's paper. The story on the right hand side.

Nick   What's it say?

Bashir (*picking up the paper again*)   It says that at the annual meeting of the Central Bankers of Pakistan on Thursday, a van filled with explosives drove into the bank and detonated, killing the Governor of the State Bank and all the members of its board . . . (*Beat.*) It says the Pakistani rupee has gone into a free fall. (*Beat.*) Remember how you were always saying the rupee was one crisis away from insolvency. (*Pointing at the paper.*) Well, there's your crisis.

Nick   Why are you telling me this?

Bashir   I invested all the capital we made into put options on the idea that the Pakistani rupee was going to drop in value . . .

Nick   How did you know –

Bashir   And then I arranged the bombing of the Central Bank of Pakistan during their policy meeting.

Nick   You did what?

Bashir (*over*)   And now that the rupee's collapsed, my position in the market's worth thirty-five million dollars. (*Beat.*) You have any idea how much good this is going to do? (*Pointing to the paper.*) It's is going to bring down the government. The time is ripe for revolution. Spring has finally come to Pakistan.

Nick   You killed all the central bankers . . .

Bashir   Ever since that thing with Bilal Ansoor – him getting hit by Lashkar, and window that gave us on the market – $700,000 in six minutes. And then, all your pestering about the rupee – well, it finally caught on at some point. He who controls the currency, controls the power, Nick. Currency is king. You taught me that.

Nick   No . . . God . . . I didn't, uh . . .

He takes up the paper, the truth slowly coming into full focus.

Bashir   Don't worry. Still no blood on your hands.

Pause.

Nick   Bashir. Please. Let me get back to work. I need to be working. I can't . . . Please. Bashir . . .

Beat.

Bashir   There must be some version of that Stockholm thing, just the other way around, if you know what I mean. Not you feeling things about me, but me feeling things about you. I think I got something like that. (*Beat.*) Way I see it, you've more than made your ransom. I'm guessing, in my shoes maybe you wouldn't do the same, but . . . You're a free man, Nick.

He gestures to **Dar** *to unlock the shackles.*

Bashir (*pointing to the open door*)   You're free to go.

He pulls out a wad of money, peels off bills.

Just be careful out there. There really is blood flowing in the streets.

Nick *takes the bills.*

As sounds of distant warfare punctuate the silence.

Nick *moves to the door. Stops. Looks back at the cell.*

Unsure. A free man.

Paralyzed.

Blackout.

Bloomsbury Methuen Drama Modern Plays

include work by

Bola Agbaje
Edward Albee
Davey Anderson
Jean Anouilh
John Arden
Peter Barnes
Sebastian Barry
Alistair Beaton
Brendan Behan
Edward Bond
William Boyd
Bertolt Brecht
Howard Brenton
Amelia Bullmore
Anthony Burgess
Leo Butler
Jim Cartwright
Lolita Chakrabarti
Caryl Churchill
Lucinda Coxon
Curious Directive
Nick Darke
Shelagh Delaney
Ishy Din
Claire Dowie
David Edgar
David Eldridge
Dario Fo
Michael Frayn
John Godber
Paul Godfrey
James Graham
David Greig
John Guare
Mark Haddon
Peter Handke
David Harrower
Jonathan Harvey
Iain Heggie

Robert Holman
Caroline Horton
Terry Johnson
Sarah Kane
Barrie Keeffe
Doug Lucie
Anders Lustgarten
David Mamet
Patrick Marber
Martin McDonagh
Arthur Miller
D. C. Moore
Tom Murphy
Phyllis Nagy
Anthony Neilson
Peter Nichols
Joe Orton
Joe Penhall
Luigi Pirandello
Stephen Poliakoff
Lucy Prebble
Peter Quilter
Mark Ravenhill
Philip Ridley
Willy Russell
Jean-Paul Sartre
Sam Shepard
Martin Sherman
Wole Soyinka
Simon Stephens
Peter Straughan
Kate Tempest
Theatre Workshop
Judy Upton
Timberlake Wertenbaker
Roy Williams
Snoo Wilson
Frances Ya-Chu Cowhig
Benjamin Zephaniah

Bloomsbury Methuen Drama Contemporary Dramatists

include

John Arden (two volumes)
Arden & D'Arcy
Peter Barnes (three volumes)
Sebastian Barry
Mike Bartlett
Dermot Bolger
Edward Bond (eight volumes)
Howard Brenton (two volumes)
Leo Butler
Richard Cameron
Jim Cartwright
Caryl Churchill (two volumes)
Complicite
Sarah Daniels (two volumes)
Nick Darke
David Edgar (three volumes)
David Eldridge (two volumes)
Ben Elton
Per Olov Enquist
Dario Fo (two volumes)
Michael Frayn (four volumes)
John Godber (four volumes)
Paul Godfrey
James Graham
David Greig
John Guare
Lee Hall (two volumes)
Katori Hall
Peter Handke
Jonathan Harvey (two volumes)
Iain Heggie
Israel Horovitz
Declan Hughes
Terry Johnson (three volumes)
Sarah Kane
Barrie Keeffe
Bernard-Marie Koltès (two volumes)
Franz Xaver Kroetz
Kwame Kwei-Armah
David Lan
Bryony Lavery
Deborah Levy
Doug Lucie

David Mamet (four volumes)
Patrick Marber
Martin McDonagh
Duncan McLean
David Mercer (two volumes)
Anthony Minghella (two volumes)
Tom Murphy (six volumes)
Phyllis Nagy
Anthony Neilson (two volumes)
Peter Nichol (two volumes)
Philip Osment
Gary Owen
Louise Page
Stewart Parker (two volumes)
Joe Penhall (two volumes)
Stephen Poliakoff (three volumes)
David Rabe (two volumes)
Mark Ravenhill (three volumes)
Christina Reid
Philip Ridley (two volumes)
Willy Russell
Eric-Emmanuel Schmitt
Ntozake Shange
Sam Shepard (two volumes)
Martin Sherman (two volumes)
Christopher Shinn
Joshua Sobel
Wole Soyinka (two volumes)
Simon Stephens (three volumes)
Shelagh Stephenson
David Storey (three volumes)
C. P. Taylor
Sue Townsend
Judy Upton
Michel Vinaver (two volumes)
Arnold Wesker (two volumes)
Peter Whelan
Michael Wilcox
Roy Williams (four volumes)
David Williamson
Snoo Wilson (two volumes)
David Wood (two volumes)
Victoria Wood

For a complete listing of Bloomsbury
Methuen Drama titles, visit:
www.bloomsbury.com/drama

Follow us on Twitter and keep up to date
with our news and publications
@MethuenDrama